Managing Employees When Turnover Is Not An Option

Table of Contents

Introduction

When it comes to industries most affected by economic upturns and downturns, the automotive service industry feels the effects first.

Recession can be a great thing for automotive service shops, for instance, as car owners tend to keep their vehicles on the road longer, thus necessitating more repairs.

Similarly, economic booms can actually be harder for automotive repair shops, as car owners are more likely to buy newer vehicles.

As a result, the most successful automotive repair shops are built to weather both the ups and the downs. That means focusing on growing customer satisfaction, improving customer retention, and making service management less frustrating. I address each of those pieces in my first book, *Service Management Made Simple*. Those are forward-facing strategies.

There are also steps you can take that are inward-facing, related to developing your business and organizational culture.

Building and retaining a loyal customer base is one of the keys to withstanding the ups-and-downs of economic cycles. And a huge part of that is dependent both on the service you provide and the organizational culture of your operation.

Customers return to places where they feel like part of a family. That doesn't happen without creating an organization that genuinely does feel like family, without creating an organization where individuals can each feel included in something larger, are valued and held accountable. In the following pages, you'll learn the lessons I've learned about creating that organizational culture based on my 29 years of experience in the automotive service industry.

Let me be blunt with you: I cannot claim to be the world's foremost expert on business or organizational culture, nor can I claim to be the world's foremost expert on the automotive service industry. In my opinion, nobody will ever be either of those things.

What I can do, though, is tell you what has worked for me and make it as easy as possible for you to implement similar strategies in your own businesses.

In writing this book, I've focused on the idea of managing when turnover is not an option because turnover is one of the most overlooked ways managers hurt their shops' culture and ability to grow. But this isn't a book just about turnover. Instead, it's a book about you: About making you the best manager you can be.

Think of it as a managerial boot camp or kick in the rear.

These are the things I want you to take away from this book:

- ***An understanding of the skills necessary to effectively manage people—and how you can get better at each of them.***
- ***An understanding of management skills that lead to positive organizational culture.***
- ***A better understanding of the people who work for you, and how to get the best from each of them.***

In writing this book, I've tried to make it as easy as possible for you to identify what is already working in your organization as well as to identify what is not. From that point, I want to help you realize what steps you need to take to make the biggest possible difference in your organizational culture.

How to use this book:

- *As you need it.*
- *Read it cover-to-cover, or flip through to the sections you need as you need them.*
- *By perusing the highlighted sections to grab the pieces you need.*
- *Write in the ample margins for future reference.*

Best practices, key ideas, and useful resources have all been called out and highlighted for easy recognition and reference. You can use this book the way that works best for you: Read it cover-to-cover, or flip through as needed, taking suggestion from various sections as applicable to your managerial process and organizational needs.

I encourage you, too, to share this book with others that may benefit from it, whether that's other business owners, members of your organization, family, or friends. I fully believe we can all use help, and we can always use more opportunities to grow and learn; hopefully others in your life feel similarly.

And lastly, don't be afraid of change. Successful business and organizational culture evolve with the needs of the organization, the changing client base, and the growth of employees and others. Take what you can from this book, combine it with your own experience, your own organization, and your own market, and adapt strategies I share here to the processes you have found work well for you. Finally, never stop learning and growing!

Chapter 1: Survival of the Fittest

If for no other reason (and there are obviously plenty of other good reasons), you need to acquire management skills because the industry is demanding it. Your shop must grow or face the chance of becoming obsolete. If your exit strategy is to close the doors and walk away when you can no longer turn a wrench (or when you have enough money in the bank to retire), then don't worry about reading any further. And while that isn't the choice I made for myself, I do understand why you might think it is the choice for you, I really do.

Do you want these things?

- *A sustainable organization.*
- *An organization you can pass on when you're ready to hang it up.*

- ***An organization that adapts with the changing market.***

If so, then you must develop your management skills.

That said, though, if you want an organization that is sustainable, can be passed along to someone else when it comes that time, and will continue to be viable in a rapidly changing business environment, then you must recognize the importance of managing people. Especially as the workforce continues to turn over and change with increasing frequency (the average person now changes jobs 12 times during their career, for instance, and the median job stay is now just more than 4 years), one of the best ways to ensure stability in your workforce is to manage well.

As a result, there's never been a time when it's been more important that shop owners and other managers learn to manage people in a positive organizational culture that creates accountability, helps communicate goals, includes clear processes, and can adapt and change as needed.

So clearly, strong management skills are what can help set your business apart, make it more appealing for prospective new hires, and convince employees to stay engaged and invested in their work for more than just a few years.

I say this to help drill home that the work of becoming a good manager is worth it. In fact, it's essential.

Hiring great technicians and having top-of-the-line equipment isn't enough. Management skills are what will set your business apart, so spend the time to develop these skills.

Managing is a mental process. It requires patience, great communication, and set processes. Rarely can a manager ever speak what needs to be done and just have it done. That simply isn't how people are wired.

(Related to this: For some managers who gravitate toward an autocratic style naturally, this can be difficult. We'll look at strategies for you in future chapters.)

Quite simply, you know how there was always that kid in school that had to ask "why" to everything the teacher said? Well, that's pretty much how everyone is at various points in their life, and that's no less true with automotive employees than in any other field.

Yes, your employees will take direction—with varying degrees of success depending on what you are asking them to do and how well they understand the why and the how of whatever it is you are asking them to do.

If you are to learn to manage in a way that allows your employees and business to grow, you must be committed to the process of learning,

practicing, reflecting, and trying a different direction.

If you are to learn to manage in a way that allows your employees and business to grow, you must be committed to the process of learning, practicing, reflecting, and trying a different direction. There is no way around the fact that managing people and organizations takes time. You will not be able to perform adequate management duties while working in the business. You must first learn to work on the business, rather than in the business.

I realize this may seem counterintuitive, especially the more mechanically-minded you may naturally be. As a result, becoming a good manager, one who is able to focus on developing the business —rather than the work the business does for clients and customers—may require a major shift in how you think about work.

If work to you means constant motion and always looking busy, such as the routine and priorities many shop owners fall into of getting cars diagnosed, fixed quickly, and out the door so another car can come in, you will likely struggle with your new management role at first. I used to love to think that it must be nice to manage—because, like many techs, it looked to me like the managers didn't do anything all day while we technicians worked our tails off. The truth is that managers work just as hard, or in the case of great managers, often much harder. What many techs don't realize—and what I didn't realize when I was a tech—is that the work often goes on between the ears rather than with the hands.

The truth is that managers work just as hard as anyone, or in the case of great managers, often much harder than others.

For many of us, that's scary. We're used to working with our hands. We're used to the way we use our brain—as if everything were a set of physics applications. Using our brains to solve people problems, though, is new for a lot of us, and as a result, it can be scary.

It doesn't have to be scary, though. These are skills you can learn. Again, though, it will take a commitment to learning, practicing, making mistakes, and trying a different approach when you realize something you tried didn't work.

In that sense, managing people is a bit of a mechanical problem. As you learn what works and what doesn't, you can think of yourself adding tools to your managerial toolbox. Over time, then, you develop skills and acquire experience just as you did as a technician, and those skills and experiences (combined with the work you do on yourself as you learn your natural management style as well as the work you do on your organizational culture) make you a better manager while you continue to grow and

19

learn and use the new skills you have at your disposal with increased experience.

Chapter 2: People Are Not Machines

In the decades I've spent in the automotive industry, I've learned a few things about cars. The biggest lesson I've learned in the past two decades, though, has been to appreciate the differences between people and machines. If you want to be a successful manager, I suspect it will be one of the biggest lessons you have to learn, too.

From personal experience, I know how easy it can be to go from fixing vehicles as an employee to owning your own shop.

I know how easy that can be because that's my story exactly. One day I was working for a guy named Ray, fixing cars and trucks, and the next I was fixing them for myself, running my own shop. It really was that simple. Customers came to the shop, work got done, and money was collected.

As time went on, though, word got out about this little shop that did great work at reasonable rates. Before I knew it, I was busy—real busy. Soon, I needed help, and so I hired my first employees.

Almost before I knew it, I needed quite a few employees, enough employees that I wasn't really working on autos anymore. Instead, I was managing a shop full of people—and so long down the road, that became managing people who were managing people.

The only problem was, none of us knew what we were doing. We could barely manage our day, much less manage people and processes. I was great at the technical stuff, great at working out mechanical problems. I always have been, and that's part of what helped me set out on my own. And quite a few of my employees, including those that also were shifted into management positions in my shop, were similarly skilled.

We're hardly alone in that regard, either. Odds are good that if you're reading this book it's because you are a similar position in your own business or organization. If I were a betting man, I'd be willing to wager this in part because you're technically and mechanically proficient (if not outright gifted) but don't necessarily know what you're doing when managing people.

And that's where we were in my shop. There was not a single individual in the organization who had ever attended a management class, much less gone through an entire program. This plays out over and over every day, month, and year in the independent repair shop industry.

People are not machines:

- **People don't play by the rules of physics; machines do.**
- **People change; the rules of physics do not.**
- **People need to be managed.**
- **People are complex: creative, selfish, helpful, and so much more.**

And managing people is significantly different than solving mechanical problems. When it comes to solving mechanical problems, there are rules you can work by. Mechanical things abide by the rules of physics, and previously solved problems can often inform any manner of new technical problems as a well. Sure, it can get a little tricky when dealing with electrical systems, for instance, or computer pieces, but the principles remain the same.

Managing people is significantly different than solving mechanical problems.

Even with the most problematic vehicles, you'll eventually find a solution if you keep at it. It may take you longer than you would like, cost some money in parts you didn't need, but you will, in time, fix the problem. Unfortunately for us technically-minded people, that's not how people work.

People don't play by the rules of physics, for instance. Instead, people seem to live by their own rules, and even when you think you've figured someone out, those rules may change from day to day based on what else is going on their life. People are challenging!

Managing, though—and especially managing well—means learning to think about what it takes to motivate people and hold people accountable. Managing means trying to understand why people do what they do, both employees and customers. Managing means putting processes in place that ensure the business moves forward even as both your employees and customers are unpredictable beings.

Managing—and especially managing well—means learning to think about what it takes to motivate people and hold people accountable.

Those processes speak to your culture, and they speak to the relationships you have both with your employees and with your customers, even as they reflect your own management style. As a result, each of you will have your own processes. What is important as a good manager is ensuring that those processes are reasonable, understood by those that need to utilize them, and that you are willing to adapt and change as new information comes to light or you get feedback that requires those changes.

Think about friends and family for a moment. Odds are good that even within your close family and friends, you can think of very different people, just as you can think of people that may act very differently in different situations depending on the context.

The truth is that human beings are creative, selfish, helpful—and so many more things.

All of these things can be true at the same time, too. Every single person is different, and each person you work with—whether an employee or a client—may prove challenging in different ways.

And all the traits and characteristics that make us wonderfully human can also work against a growing business. There are days when we need our employees to be more creative, just as there may be days when we wish they were not so creative!

One day we might find ourselves incredibly frustrated by their seeming inability to just follow directions while in that same week we may find ourselves wishing an employee would work more autonomously and just do what needs to be done.

Truthfully, most people are selfish and self-serving, yet this can be combined with a wonderful sense of helpfulness and kindness. Some of our human employees are great thinkers, while others can only seem to follow very specific directions. All of these traits we need from our employees in order to create an adaptable and skilled team—and yet those same attributes can create havoc when we least expect.

Managing a team well means using these traits to our advantage and keeping the less than desirable traits from sinking our ship and chasing all our customers (or other employees) away.

And, I promise, it's often far harder than it sounds. So why do we do it? Quite simply because if we want our businesses to be successful, we don't have a choice.

If we want our business to grow, we have to manage it and the people that make it run.

Defining Management

One of the definitions of management I've loved most is as follows:

Noun
1. The process of dealing with or controlling things or people.
"The management of elk herds."
2. ARCHAIC trickery; deceit.
"If there has been any management in the business, it has been concealed from me."

I loved this definition when I found it—especially the archaic definition of "trickery and deceit." This certainly summed up my opinion of managers when I was working in larger organizations. They always seemed to be trying anything they could to get me to produce more, do more for less, do more with less, or just plain get me to work every possible minute of the day. The problem was that I had very few managers who could manage and even fewer who wanted to learn to manage.

You cannot bend someone to your will and get the outcome you expect.

I disagree with the definition of management being "controlling"—and to be completely frank, I hope you disagree with that model of management, too. Instead, I would prefer to think of management as "guiding to an acceptable outcome." In my experience, there is very little actual control when it comes to managing people. You cannot bend

27

someone to your will and get the outcome you expect. That's just not how people work.

Learning To Manage

Of course, just because your brain might naturally gravitate toward technical and mechanical solutions doesn't mean you cannot learn how to manage people and, in fact, if you want your organization to successfully grow you must do precisely that.

Does becoming a great manager require a different set of skills than fixing an engine? Definitely! But that hardly means it cannot be done. Management skills require a different way of thinking, but it is a way of thinking that can—and should—be learned.

> *Management skills require a different way of thinking, but it is a way of thinking that can—and should—be learned.*

I understand that managing people probably isn't what you had in mind when you opened your shop. It certainly wasn't what I was thinking about when I first started. Maybe you just acquired your shop because you were next in line and the opportunity presented itself—I know this is how plenty of automotive service people have ended up running their first shop, and there's nothing wrong with that. Regardless of how you got to where you are today, though, and regardless of how little you may have thought about management skills before, you are now managing a

28

shop full of employees—and you need to think long and hard about what that means.

No matter where your mindset is today, no matter how adaptable you think you are, I can almost guarantee you will have to continue challenging yourself—and how you naturally think about things—to become a better manager.

But you can do this. All too often I hear shop owners say how hard it is to hire good people. It is! They would have to hire less often, or be able to hire less-than-perfect employees, if they were to develop stronger management skills. We live and work in a world today where there is no option other than to learn to become a great manager of people. Don't think for a second that not growing, staying small, or not purchasing that other shop location is okay because you "just don't have the management to do it."

Instead, embrace the challenge. You can and will learn to think differently, speak differently, work differently, and you will, with time and practice, begin to understand how to get the most out of the people you have working for you.

And frankly, you don't have much of a choice.

If you want to survive, and thrive, in this industry, you have to acquire management skills.

Chapter 3: Building Business Processes

You must learn to work on the business—rather than in the business. This cannot be overemphasized. Let me say that again....YOU MUST learn to work ON your business, not IN your business. Managing is about working on the business.

When you first decide that you must spend each day working on the business, rather than in it, you may struggle with what to do every day. If you are used to always being involved in the work being done, whether that be diagnosing problem vehicles, executing repairs, or dealing with customers, you will find this a significant challenge. If you're like me, your natural inclination is to jump behind the counter to help out whenever you see the need, or to dive into the shop when it seems like they could use an extra hand—or when it looks like an employee might need

31

an extra set of eyes and your experience to improve their diagnostics, you will find yourself fighting your own instincts for a while.

> ### *As a manager, it is your job to work on the business—not in the business.*

But here's the thing: Even as you are trying to help things run smoothly and efficiently, you may actually be hurting your business. As an owner or manager whose job it is to keep the business rolling and growing, you hold the business back by jumping in, even if that may help you at that very moment. Instead, you need to hire the best people you can and get out of the way.

> ### *Even as you are trying to help things run smoothly and efficiently, you may actually be hurting your business.*

Let your employees learn and become more efficient with experience. Guide them, sure, but don't micromanage them or do their work for them.

Instead, if you really want the business to grow, you need to focus your energy on putting structures in place to help make that growth achievable and sustainable.

> ### *As an owner or manager, your experience is more valuable when you put your time and energy into developing a great team of employees.*

As an owner or manager, your experience is more valuable when you put your time and energy into developing a great team of employees (which means hiring wisely and then building the infrastructure to help keep them engaged, satisfied, and productive) and a great structure and culture for growth. This means focusing your energy on processes, on policy, on guidelines for what the growth should look like.

This means you have processes and procedures for hiring, on-boarding, and training new employees, for intaking and retaining clients. This means you have support structures in place to help employees who might be struggling with new skills, for instance, or for those that just want to learn, grow, and be the best they can be.

Building a framework that makes growth and expansion possible and sustainable is better use of your time and energy than doing your employees' work for them, as tempting as jumping behind the counter or into the shop is.

Our goal should be to manage people. We want to set ourselves, our employees, and our business up for success. That means creating a culture where turnover is minimal, we hire for organizational fit, and we understand that it is on us to train and support our employees to keep fireable offenses to a minimum. As an owner or manager, you are far better off creating an organization that sets people up for success, rather than one that relies strictly on hiring the best, time after time. (No, there's nothing wrong with hiring the best, it's just an inefficient business strategy in times of low unemployment or difficult-to-find skill sets). After all, do you really want to keep replacing people because you didn't hire the right person the first time, or didn't set that person up with the skills and support they needed to be successful?

Posting ads, interviewing, hiring, on-boarding, evaluating, and then having to do it all over again and again takes, and wastes, too much valuable time.

Bare minimum business processes for a truly sustainable organization:

- ***Formal interviewing process(es).***
- ***Onboarding process(es).***
- ***Mentoring programs for all employees.***
- ***Formal employee review process(es).***
- ***Great internal communication.***

A truly sustainable organization, one that sets people up for success, has formal management processes that include an interviewing process, onboarding process, mentoring program for all employees, formal employee review process, and great internal communication. All of this together creates a positive culture where turnover is minimized and the need to hire constantly is reduced.

As you dive deeper into your organizational culture, you may find other places where you can improve as well, but the aforementioned list is a bare minimum when it comes to setting up your organization for success.

Chapter 4: Basics of Managing People

Let's start with some of the basic management skills you'll need to master to effectively manage your team.

The following is hardly a complete list, but it is a starting point. Consider these the building blocks you'll want as you develop your managerial skills.

Managerial building blocks 101:

- ***Clearly setting expectations.***
- ***Consistent and effective communication.***
- ***Objectivity (and a willingness to set aside bias/recognize your own emotions).***
- ***Actively listening.***
- ***Coaching.***
- ***Consistency in application.***

Consider this chapter an overview, especially as we'll dive into greater depth in future chapters. This is a starting point, though, the bare minimum of what you will need in order to be successful. The list above is distilled from a much longer list based on my professional observations, personal experiences, and formal management training.

You don't have to learn these skills all at once, and in fact, trying to do so may prove impossible. Instead, recognize that mastery of these skills is a life-long process, understand that they are skills you will continually need to practice, and accept that even as you master these skills, there will still be times you find yourself disappointed by an employee or your inability to get through to them.

Let's spend a little bit of time examining each of these important managerial skills so you can understand precisely why they are so important. Again, keep in mind that how effective you are with each skill will vary depending on the context of the situation, your own experience and previously developed skills, as well as how each skill fits into your natural managerial style. Managing people is not and cannot be a one-size-fits-all approach, so you will need to find what works for you and tailor your methods appropriately.

Managing people is not and cannot be a one-size-fits-all approach.

In any context, though, these are the skills you must master to effectively work with and manage your teams.

Clear Expectations

It is hard for anyone to fulfill their job duties if they don't know what expectations accommodate those duties. This is true at any age and in any position. Think back to when you were in school: Which teachers were most effective? I'm guessing you might agree that it was those teachers that clearly communicated their expectations of you and detailed how you could fulfill their expectations in your work.

You may not think of yourself as a teacher, but as a manager, you are exactly that. You are both a teacher and a coach. You set the standard for your shop and for your people.

A huge part of setting that standard as a teacher, coach, and manager is setting clear expectations.

When you have employees learning a new skill, for instance, they need to know exactly how you measure success. They need to know exactly what constitutes a good job and what is an example of a job not done well. All of this needs to be clearly communicated (more on communication in a bit).
 For some managers, clearly defined standards (such as a rubric you might use for performing employee

evaluations, for instance) can be helpful in demonstrating for employees exactly what expectations you have of them.

What do I mean by a rubric? Some teachers use rubrics with their students to help their students know exactly what the expectations for an assignment might be.

Rubrics usually contain:

- *Evaluative criteria.*
- *Quality definitions for those criteria at particular levels of achievement.*
- *Scoring strategy.*

Most often presented in a table format, they can both be used by teachers when marking and by students when planning their work. As managers are teachers, they can be a great tool for communicating expectations. Even better, rubrics have been shown to have a positive impact on learning—which means they can be a great tool for you as a manager.

For other managers, demonstrations are more helpful, as are developing a mentor program where more experienced employees can help communicate expectations to new hires.

You'll need to find what method of communicating clear expectations works best for you and your team.

This may take some trial and error, but it is well worth the work.

Employees that know what work is expected of them are far more likely to accomplish that work in a way that meets your standards than workers who are left to guess at what you want from them.

Consistent and Effective Communication

Of course, one of the biggest pieces of effectively communicating expectations is making sure that your communication is consistent, clear, and effective. For different managers that may take different shapes. For some managers, it may mean regular one-on-one meetings with employees. For others, it may mean regular check-ins with mentoring employees to determine the best ways to effectively communicate messages and expectations to other employees. Again, this will be a matter of trial and error until you find what works best for you, your team, and your own managerial style.

Objectivity

It's easy to say you can be objective. It is far more difficult to actually maintain objectivity, however, especially when it comes to matters about which you are passionate.

And if you're like me, the entire reason you got into running your own shop is that it is something you are passionate and care deeply about. If you're running your own business, you're not doing it because it's easy; instead, you're a business owner because you care about your work, are passionate about what you and your employees do, and cannot imagine a different life for yourself.

Of course, that passion can also make it difficult to see things without bias or emotions. And while that passion can be a great thing as a manager—your passion for your work can be contagious, and that energy can in and of itself be an important part of your organizational culture—it can also be a complicating factor.

For instance, if you see work done in your shop that is subpar, it can be easy to get angry. After all, that isn't the kind of work you stand for, nor is it the kind of work you want customers and clients to get when they come to your shop.

But here's the thing: If you lose your cool and let that anger out on your employee, you are not able to objectively understand why the work was subpar, nor are you able to address the subpar work in a way that both allows that employee to own their mistakes and improve in the future.

You need to be able to calmly communicate where their work wasn't up to snuff.

Instead, you need to be able to calmly communicate where their work wasn't up to snuff, explain what issues need to be addressed better in the future and how their work didn't meet those expectations. If you can do this calmly, without losing your cool, it can be a teaching moment.

And teaching moments are a way to improve the culture of your organization. Allowing employees the opportunity to grow and learn from their mistakes is a hallmark of positive organizational cultures, and you can help set the tone by calmly addressing mistakes rather than losing your cool.

One caveat: Some offenses and mistakes are and should be automatic firing offenses. You'll need to determine for yourself what constitutes a mistake or error that warrants and requires firing, but every manager will have their own line.

You'll need to determine for yourself what constitutes a mistake or error that warrants and requires firing, but every manager will have their own line.

For myself, I think it comes down to a matter of safety; mistakes that could cause physical harm to other employees or clients cannot be tolerated. Nor, for that matter, can illegal activities. You, of course, will need to determine what can be corrected and what cannot.

Actively Listening

We'll spend more time with active listening in future chapters, but let's consider this an introductory primer, as it's one of the best ways to get a sense for the culture of your organization, as well as how each employee is functioning within that culture. You'll need to practice your active listening skills to continue developing your skills.

All too often we engage in selective listening. We're busy, and there are demands on our time. We may be thinking through to-do lists or working out a response to keep the conversation moving so we can move on to the next thing, rather than fully listening. This is a wholly natural human response, but it does our employees a disservice and shows a lack of respect for what they have to say.

Instead, one of the signs of a great manager is a willingness to really listen. Really hear what people have to tell you and come to conversations with a sense of curiosity and openness.

Five questions for self-reflection:

1) *Do you stop yourself from deciding in advance what people are going to say?*
2) *Do you listen with a curious and inquisitive mindset?*
3) *Do you actively seek different perspectives?*

4) Do you manage stress so you can still effectively listen?

5) Do you listen to what you hear?

Consider these five questions for self-reflection:

1) *Do you stop yourself from deciding in advance what people are going to say?* All too often we anticipate rather than really listening, and when we do this, we're not really listening in a meaningful way.

2) *Do you listen with a curious and inquisitive mindset?* All too often we listen from a place of judgment rather than from a place of curiosity. We look for reasons why there might be something wrong with what our employees or customers are telling us, rather than simply being willing to ask questions with an open mind. When we hear people with an open mind, they're more likely to be honest, open, and authentic with us. When we listen from a place of judgment, however, they're more likely to respond with defensiveness. That's not the tone or culture we want.

3) *Do you actively seek different perspectives?* This can help us break out of our ruts and help us see things in your organization in a new way, whether that's refining your culture, developing and adapting processes, or even simply seeing ways you might modify your customer service routines.

4) *Do you manage stress so you can still effectively listen?* When I work with other managers, I often see that stress is keeping them from really hearing what they're being told or from actively listening, because the stress is leading them to always focus on what's next, rather than listening in the moment.
5) *Do you listen to what you hear?* That is, do you fully listen and listen fully?

Actively listening is something that does not come naturally to most people and requires practice. As you develop your skills, however, you'll find that it makes a huge difference in your ability to communicate and affect the culture in your organization. Listening is what opens up all sorts of possibilities for you as a manager, so don't be discouraged at the amount of work it may take to fully develop this skill. Keep at it, and you'll find your skills will come around.

Coaching

Part of being a good manager is helping your team grow and develop new or better skills, and that means you need to get better at both teaching and coaching.

I include both of these skills because beyond just teaching your new techs individual skills, you also must help them develop existing skills to the point where they are finely tuned. Coaching is different than teaching and is a skill maybe more rare in the workplace today. It is an indispensable skill set to develop though. Learning to coach is sometimes more challenging than learning to teach. Good coaching will allow employees to become more efficient and skilled in each of their tasks, and even work up to the point where they can mentor and help develop new hires as they gain experience.

Coaching is one of the skills that separate good managers from great.

Coaching is one of the skills that separate good managers from great. Develop your coaching skills and you'll be amazed at just how capable your team proves.

Even better, coaching allows you the opportunity to apply the other skills you are working on this chapter.

Good coaching is a mix of clear expectations, effective communication, feedback, and active listening.

Good coaching is a mix of clear expectations, effective communication, feedback, and actively listening so you can adapt your strategy to the needs of the individuals you're coaching. We'll discuss coaching in more depth in future chapters, but it's good to start thinking about it now.

Consistency in Application

Finally, one of the last building block skills you will absolutely need to work on to become a great manager is consistency in application. If your expectations are clear, you have effectively communicated those expectations, and you have coached your team up, you can still run into issues if you are not consistent in your enforcement or expectations or in how you treat team members.

Lack of consistency can often look like favoritism or an application of personal bias, and that seeming unprofessionalism can undercut everything else you have to say.

As managers, we lead by example, and a huge part of that example is plain, straightforward consistency.

We want our employees to get the same treatment from us both on our good days and on our bad days, just as we want our clients to get the same service regardless of what may be going on in our employees' lives.

So focus on being consistent. Toward that end, asking a few trusted employees to let you know when they see examples of inconsistencies can both help hold you accountable to your team and demonstrate that you really are listening to what they have to say, and don't hold yourself above your team.

Chapter 5: Idiosyncratic People

Of course, just as we struggle with consistency, so do other people. People aren't a physics problem or a mechanical issue, which may be what we're used to. Any time we are working with people, we need to remember this. That they aren't a mechanical issue, that they aren't consistent, that they don't follow set rules.

We, as people, are all very complex beings, and each of us brings to our workplace both our skills and our challenges.

This is just as true for our employees as it is for us. Just as our strengths can be invaluable, so too can our weaknesses frustrate both ourselves and others.

As a result, each day can be different when it comes to managing people. Any number of variables can pop up daily that will make managing a new adventure. Sometimes these variables are obvious, yet many times they may not be. If an employee is truly sick and won't be coming to work for a few days, you can usually tell. If an employee just doesn't seem to be able to follow directions or be consistent in their job responsibilities, you may not be able to discern what the problem may be. It could be a lack of training, a lack of understanding the reason why, a learning disability, or a distraction from their personal life. Your management skill will determine whether the situation gets better or worse.

Of course, there are ways you can alleviate some of these problems, and the building block skills we discussed in the previous chapter are a huge part of that.

Managing is easier if:

- **Your hiring process improves.**
- **Your interviewing process improves.**
- **Your onboarding process is formalized.**
- **Employee performance is regularly reviewed.**
- **You work to earn and keep respect.**

To recap, there are simple concrete steps you can take (in addition to building up those building block skills) that can help you account for those idiosyncrasies of working with ever-changing and dynamic people.

Improving Your Hiring Process

Managing gets much easier if there is a formal process in place for hiring the best people and interviewing these potential new hires. One way to build up this process is to take notes after every interview about what went well and what didn't, and then adapt and revise based on those notes.

In particular, I recommend looking through my Interviewing Skills addendum to help you develop the process that will work best for you.

Improving Your Onboarding

It can be even easier for you to introduce new hires to your culture and your process if there is an onboarding process in place as well. This onboarding process should help familiarize new hires with the skills they will need to master, the way workflow operates in your organization, and their place in the organizational culture, among whatever other pieces you realize over time need to be introduced to new hires to help them fit more seamlessly into your organization.

In particular, I recommend looking through my Building Your Onboarding Skills addendum to help you develop the process that will work best for you.

Improving Your Performance Review Process

Once you've hired and on-boarded well, you're off to a good start. Combine this with a yearly employee review process that includes goal setting and accountability to performance, and the job of a manager can be more streamlined. Performance reviews can and should be something you're continually looking to improve, both for your sake and your employees' sake.

I encourage you to begin the review process as soon as possible. A formal review process includes:

1. A documented evaluation of an employee's performance in specific areas.
2. Comments related to employee's areas of improvement.
3. Goal setting for the next quarter (or longer).
4. An overall numerical score upon which performance increases in pay can be calculated.

It may seem overwhelming to begin this process, however, it will pay immediate dividends once you do. If you need help with suggested documentation or getting started, you can contact me through www.rsrcoach.com and we'll get you started!

Earning Respect

And of course, throughout all of this, you must work to earn respect. Employees will rarely ever just respect someone for a title—especially if that person sits in an office all day and nobody really knows what they do with that time! And that's where those building block skills we discussed really come in handy.

Remember those building block skills?

- *Clearly setting expectations.*
- *Consistent and effective communication.*
- *Objectivity (and a willingness to set aside bias/recognize your own emotions).*
- *Actively listening.*
- *Coaching.*
- *Consistency in application.*

While you could and should concentrate on developing all of those building block skills, choose two skills from the list to work on to start. If you want to choose three, feel free. Pick the two (or three) that you feel would have the most immediate benefit to you and your organization. Remember, too, that just because you learn the skill doesn't mean you won't have to continually work on it. You'll be able to give it less time in the future than you did when you were new at it, but you'll never be wholly finished with the skill development part of becoming a great manager because there is always room for improvement. None of us will ever be perfect, but that doesn't mean we shouldn't try.

I want you to identify those two to three skills you want to focus on to start right now. Write them down, and take a few moments to decide where you want to start with each.

Got it? Good.

One place to start might be setting expectations, as we discussed in the previous chapter. After all, if you don't set expectations, your employees will. That's human nature. And wouldn't you rather you were the one setting the tone?

If you don't set expectations, everyone will set their own.

If you don't set expectations, everyone will set their own—and they will all be different, just as each of your employees is different. That sets you up for a cultural fail, too, as you can't all be on the same page if each and every individual is setting their own expectations. Humans move toward and become that which they think about, and that's immediately clear in workplaces where clear expectations are not set or communicated.

If you don't set expectations with or for others, they will set their own expectations. We talk about this with customers in the customer service environment, but it holds true for employees as well. As an organization, it is extremely important that everyone holds similar expectations regarding certain core functions of the business. Otherwise, each person will set their own expectations and they may be drastically different. Even if they are not all that different, varying expectations will not lend themselves to organizational consistency.

Varying expectations do not lend themselves to organizational consistency.

Similarly, what are you always thinking about? Growing the business? Increasing customer satisfaction? Getting into a different business? If you hold these thoughts consistently enough, your actions will reflect that train of thought and you will move in that direction. I often say that every automotive service business I've ever seen was built in the image of its owner. This is due to the very fact that we move toward and become that which we think about. If fixing vehicles is most important to the owner, I often find a well-equipped shop full of work, but a poor customer waiting area, little marketing, and even less management. If customer satisfaction is most important to an owner, I often find a beautiful waiting area, well-dressed employees, good quality but low production, and low gross profits.

As people and employees, we move toward and become that which we think about.

Consistently thinking in the same direction as employees and as an organization will help to create a growing, sustainable business. As a manager, you must be very intentional about what direction things are going in and be very intentional about setting a consistent expectation.

This is especially true because of how different we are all as unique human beings. It is up to you as a manager to help channel those differences toward common goals by setting clear expectations and developing a clearly-defined organizational culture.

Thinking in the same direction means:

- ***Setting expectations.***
- ***Having a core organizational philosophy.***
- ***Holding employees accountable to expectations.***

If an organization is to think similarly or in the same direction, it must understand expectations, have an overarching philosophy to guide expectations, and be able to hold employees accountable to those expectations. Setting expectations and holding people accountable to those expectations can be time-consuming without a core organizational philosophy. A core organizational philosophy can be thought of as a single, overall expectation to be used in decision-making. If developed and implemented properly, this can reduce some of the burdens on management in terms of setting expectations and ensuring decisions are well made.

We'll discuss core organizational philosophies further in Chapter 12, but consider this a starting point to start thinking about what guides your organization.

A core organizational philosophy can be thought of as a single, overall expectation to be used in decision-making.

Chapter 6: Recognizing Your Current Workplace Culture

Why is workplace culture important? Because it translates into dollars and cents. It also translates into easier hiring and better employee retention.

For instance, Paul J. Zak and other researchers who have looked at the effects of working in high-trust organizations, for instance, have hard data to prove how valuable that environment can be. Consider some of these more staggering statistics: Employees in high-trust organization display 106 percent more energy at work, 50 percent more productivity, 74 percent less stress, and take 13 percent fewer sick days. Just as important, those same high-trust culture employees were 76 percent more engaged and 29 percent more satisfied with their jobs and overall lives. Those are not small numbers—and you and I can both imagine and know how they translate to bottom-line sales in terms of dollars and cents, too.

So use this chapter as a reminder of the importance of getting to know your culture, celebrating its strengths and addressing its weaknesses. It's worth it, even as it may take significant investigation and investment of time and energy to start.

Just remember this as you get started: Managing people is never an easy thing to do. It will be a constant work in process. People can be just plain weird…and frustrating! Understanding what your limitations are, where your strengths lay, and what you need to develop for management tools will help you become the manager you need to be.

Developing a positive workplace culture helps you to not only manage people but also makes hiring easier, allows the organization to function more on its own, and results in attracting great customers. Positive culture allows the business to grow in the direction it needs to—and often without any additional marketing activity; great workplace culture leads to the sort of business that gets word-of-mouth referrals.

With a great workplace culture, you'll find great employees will be attracted to the organization without having to go digging for them in the classifieds. Those great employees will attract more and more customers. An understanding of how people operate, what motivates them, and how to get the best from them will allow you to develop the management skills you need to run the organization at the highest level possible.

With a great workplace culture, you'll find great employees will be attracted to the organization without having to go digging for them in the classifieds.

Of course, that's all much easier said than done. To develop a positive workplace culture—or even to simply maintain a positive workplace culture, should you find you already have one—you first have to recognize and appreciate your current workplace culture for what it is.

And that means paying attention. Some parts of your organizational culture will be apparent enough to you if you simply spend some time observing how your workplace works. Others, however, will require you to ask your employees questions—and then you must really listen to the answers.

As a manager, you often must address workplace issues that may arise in your organization.

Oftentimes, those issues arise from some sort of cultural disconnect—some place where there is a gap between the culture of your organization and what you and/or the conflicting employees want and/or need.

Examining Your Culture Objectively

As a manager, you are steeped in your workplace culture, saturated by it. How do you step back and take an objective look at a culture in which you play a huge role?

One way to take a more objective look at your organizational culture is to think of yourself as a cultural detective.

Just like an effective detective, to get at the center of your organizational culture you must be observant. You must also be self-aware (which is where learning to recognize your managerial style comes in handy - we'll discuss this in a little bit), curious (willing to follow a question's natural thread back to a source), and a good, active listener.

Attributes of a cultural detective:

- *Self-aware.*
- *Curious.*
- *Active listener.*

Let's take some time to explore each of those points, starting with the last point first.

Active Listening

If a detective asks a question but isn't fully invested in listening to the answer—including seeing that answer from the perspective of the person responding to their questions—they are likely to miss information, including observations, data, or viewpoints that could be key to solving the case. The same is true for you as a manager: If you are not a skilled and active listener, your observational skills and curiosity can only take you so far.

When I work with other managers to help them better understand the culture of their shop, I especially make a point to emphasize this: Listening is one of the keys to understanding your workplace culture and the needs of your employees, as well as to implementing change effectively. If we can't listen, we cannot communicate nor self-reflect—both of which are essential parts of growth, both for ourselves and for others and especially for our culture.

If we can't listen, we cannot communicate nor self-reflect—both of which are essential parts of growth.

Listening is the basis of empathy, growth, and learning, so if we cannot listen well, we really cannot do much at all to help our team. And listening is not that hard! Listening is simply allowing words to enter your ears and then your brain.

Better yet, listening closely is a form of respect and connection.

Good listening communicates that we hear, acknowledges the other person, shows we believe what they have to say is important, and confers our respect for them.

Listening is the starting point of communication with others, and rarely is this more powerful than as a manager who wants to convey how you value your employees.

As a manager, you are uniquely positioned to hear a wide variety of voices, too, both from the full range of employees working under your command and from customers and clients. Consider each perspective as you listen to what people have to tell you, and see your workplace and organization through their eyes.

And if this is something you struggle with at first, that's okay. We'll talk about improving your active listening skills more in coming chapters as well.

Observation

As a manager and as a detective, observing how people interact in your workplace can also provide numerous clues as you explore the underlying culture. Watch how employees interact during meetings, what they choose to discuss during informal conversations, what their body language states about how they are feeling. Watch how clients and customers interact with your employees. Are they happy to see a friendly face, or is visiting your business something they dread?

Practice your observation skills and you may be surprised by what you are able to learn about your organization's culture.

Watch for patterns of behavior in groups that shed light on how your culture operates. For instance, which meetings are productive and which aren't? What are people comfortable and uncomfortable expressing? Where are they comfortable expressing opinions, and where are they not? (i.e. Do they use email or texting to express opinions, or do they do so openly?). Why might they be uncomfortable expressing a particular opinion, experience, or belief? What does that discomfort say about the larger cultural system? Similarly, what are they passionate about and why? Practice your observation skills and you may be surprised by what you are able to learn about your organization's culture, just as a detective may unlock larger truths by careful, objective observation.

Self-Awareness

This is where recognizing who you naturally are as a manager comes in handy. If you can recognize your own biases, you can recognize the places that those biases may color your perceptions of the people and situations around you, including how you listen to them and how much stock you put in what they tell us. For instance, if you think of someone as a complainer then you are likely to regard their viewpoint as irrelevant, even though they may have important feedback to share. Good detectives—and good managers—step outside of their own biases because they are aware of them.

Be aware of any tendencies to extrapolate or make assumptions based on the information or feedback you receive.

Curiosity

This goes back to listening, too. Asking good questions is the foundation of curiosity. Perhaps you've heard someone say there's no such thing as a bad question. That's not entirely true. But there is no such thing as a bad authentic question. If you're not exercising the art of curiosity, it's difficult to ask authentic questions. And if you're not asking authentic questions, it's hard to meet people where they are and see things from their perspective.

Consider different questions you might hear in your organization's meetings or even in informal conversations you may have with other members of your team or with your employees: How many of those questions are rooted in curiosity (and the genuine desire to know something), and how many of them are instead questions disguised as a way to showcase the speaker's own viewpoints (such as rhetorical or leading questions)?

All too often, organizational conversations inadvertently and unintentionally deemphasize curiosity.

Instead, people ask leading questions, questions in which they already have an answer in mind, questions like "Do you enjoy working here?" Leading questions have a clear answer in mind; either the employee likes working here, or the implication is that perhaps they'd be better off finding somewhere else to work. And that's hardly the only leading question managers might ask.

Think about this from your own experience: Do you feel heard when someone is asking you leading questions? In your interview experience (whether interviewing or being interviewed), have you noted the difference between interviews that feel like a conversation—where it's clear the person asking the questions is genuinely interested in the answer—and interviews full of leading questions, where there is clearly a right or wrong answer?

This is again a place where being aware of your managerial style can help you supplement your own questioning style with questions that may be more conducive to helping people feel heard, such as questions that are more open-ended and which force you to listen with a sense of curiosity.

Instead of asking a leading question such as "Do you enjoy working here," perhaps you learn to ask employees the pros and cons of their current position, or what they're good at and what they might need to improve. Leave your questions open-ended and you're more likely to get valuable information out of the question.

Cultural Interviewing

This next step may not be for everyone, but as a manager trying to get a sense for your organizational culture, you may wish to actually interview stakeholders in that culture, whether formally or informally. Of course, if you do choose to do this, you must do it right. Ask questions from a place of curiosity, and do so with an open-minded desire to learn.

I use the online tool www.ultigoal.com, for instance, to help the organizations I work with anonymously evaluate organizational culture.

When I'm looking at organizational culture, I have several go-to questions that are intentionally open-ended.

I like these questions because they force me—or whoever is doing the interviewing—to be open-minded and meet people where they are. Before I begin asking these questions, I make it clear that these interviews are confidential and clarify how the answers will be used; you will want to do the same. (And if you don't get the sense that employees will be as truthful with you as their manager, consider bringing someone in to do the interviewing and compiling of data for you.) For instance, if you are asking people these questions to identify pain points, process bottlenecks, and opportunities for improvement in your organization's cultural systems, you must be transparent with your interviewees. Any other approach will increase mistrust, frustration, and disengagement.

Let's look at these questions one at a time.

- *What are the bright spots in your culture?*

Starting from a positive place allows you to work from shared common ground and can help you develop a connection. Additionally, because this question is open-ended, it allows your interviewee to focus on the places most important to them, which in and of itself can tell you things about the organizational culture.

- *What are the points of tension?*

It may be worth clarifying that these points of tension could be between people, could be points of a system, or may be issues or processes that are causing them personal tension. You are focusing on ensuring that your questions are not leading, but rather allow individuals to answer honestly and openly.

- *If I gave you a magic wand, what three changes would you make?*

Because this is a magic wand, it grants the power, authority, and resources to make the suggested changes; the point here isn't to look at reasons why you can't do something, but rather things you could do to improve the organization and organizational culture if there weren't any limitations.

Your goal here is to understand the culture and what parts of that culture need to change, rather than say why it can't change. Likewise, your attitude as you ask these questions can make a big difference, too.

Your attitude as you ask these questions can make a big difference, too, in how your people respond. Ask your questions impartially, curiously, and in a one-on-one setting to ensure openness, transparency, and honesty. Respect confidentiality and ask follow-up questions as needed to fully hear what people tell you, and you'll be well on your way to fully understanding your organizational culture—which can, in turn, help you identify its strengths and weaknesses, as well as begin developing a plan for improving it as needed.

The importance of setting the right attitude and being willing to really listen is true for both employees and customers, but the way you model those behaviors will set the tone for your organization. Asking real questions that can get at the heart of your organizational culture can be petrifying, but it can also be tremendously rewarding if you are willing to listen inquisitively and curiously, and are willing to act on what you hear.

Employees prefer working with, and for, managers who want to hear what they have to say and value their input. Customers likewise appreciate business owners and employees who hear what they have to say. Just know, however, that if you do not really hear what you are told, do not actively listen, or do not act on what you learn, you will lose the power you originally gain by asking.

There are many other questions to consider that are equally open-ended and can also help you understand the culture of your organization. Pick and choose from the list below to find the questions that best fit your needs.

Open-ended cultural detective questions to consider:

- *What are the bright spots in your culture?*
- *What are the points of tension in your organization?*
- *If I gave you a magic wand, what three changes would you make?*
- *What are people talking about in your organization? How are they talking about it?*
- *What's the emotional culture? What are people allowed to express—and what gets suppressed?*
- *What behaviors are tolerated? What behaviors get rewarded?*
- *How are decisions made? Who makes them and how?*
- *How is trust built? How would you describe the level of trust?*
- *How is conflict handled? What types of conflict do you observe in the organization?*
- *What are the barriers to collaboration?*
- *How do people relate and connect? Is it by organizational hierarchy, or in other ways?*

Obviously, some of these questions may be more relevant for your organization than others. You can also tailor your own questions to better reflect what you feel you need to know about your organizational culture, especially if you are willing to change those questions as you get more feedback and gather relevant information from others.

I can recommend a few strategies to help you stay organized as you gather this information and ask these questions in your one-on-one interviews, whether they are formal or informal.

First, I would recommend compiling the information you gather from each individual separately. Ask them to verify that you understand their responses and concerns appropriately, based on your notes. As needed, amend your notes to better reflect how they feel.

Second, I would recommend pulling together all those insights into one document. After ensuring you have removed any information that might identify respondents, share your findings with others in the organization that are in a position to help verify your findings (department heads, or those with certain areas of responsibility, for instance, may be a good start here). As you compile your findings, look for trends and themes. What in your interviews have emerged as areas for further investigation? What concerns or feedback do people consistently mention?

As a manager, I recognize this may be a tremendous amount of information through which to sort, especially as you may (and likely do) already feel overworked. I know there are a great number of demands on your time and of your energy, and spending the time it takes to not only conduct these cultural investigation interviews but then verify and compile the results can feel tremendously overwhelming. I get it.

I also know from experience, however, how valuable such an investigation into your organizational culture can be. If it isn't something you feel you can afford the time and energy to do yourself—but you still recognize that you could use a better understanding of your organizational culture—consider bringing in a third-party to help you with this process.

Organizational consultants are not generally cheap, but being able to gather this information and then act on it can be a tremendous boon to really developing your organizational culture so that your business can grow and thrive well into the future.

Gathering this information gives you a wealth of knowledge from which you can look at your organization objectively, removed from your inherent biases, consequently allowing you to see the culture of your workplace for what it is.

If you can gather those clues and put the pieces together in a coherent fashion that reflects self-awareness and objectivity, you can then build on that information.

The first step toward improving your organizational culture is recognizing it in its current form so you can best identify strengths and weaknesses.

Only after you identify strengths and weaknesses can you develop a plan for improvement.
Implementing that plan is another step, and as you make changes, you can likely expect some resistance. That's okay. Change is often scary for everyone involved.

As before, it will be important that you get feedback regularly, listen to people both inside and outside the system when they tell you what is and isn't working, and adjust accordingly.

And know that addressing your culture is worth it, as we discussed previously. You saw the statistics. Make the changes to your organizational culture and you'll see the returns.

Paul J. Zak and other researchers who have looked at the effects of working in high-trust organizations, for instance, have hard data to prove it. Consider some of these more staggering statistics: Employees in high-trust organization display 106 percent more energy at work, 50 percent more productivity, 74 percent less stress, and take 13 percent fewer sick days. Just as important, those same high-trust culture employees were 76 percent more engaged and 29 percent more satisfied with their jobs and overall lives. Those are not small numbers—and you and I can both imagine and know how they translate to bottom-line sales in terms of dollars and cents, too.

So take the time to get to know your culture, celebrating its strengths and addressing its weaknesses. It's worth it, even as it may take significant investigation and investment of time and energy to start. Start by asking questions, follow-through on what you learn, continually revisit and revise as needed, and you'll have a fantastic and positive work culture in your organization before you know it.

Know, too, that even if this feels a bit abstract right now, that's okay. We'll talk more about what a positive workplace culture might look like in concrete details in coming chapters as we discuss the different skills you'll need to be a great manager, based both on my experience and the experiences of other managers just like you. Until then, though, I still want this percolating in your mind as you read the materials I have to share with you in the pages and chapters ahead.

Chapter 7: The True Cost of Turnover

Okay, you might be saying, I get that there are places where I can improve as a manager. You also likely understand intuitively what a difference improving your organizational culture can make.

For many managers, however, it can be difficult at first to understand where limiting—if not outright eliminating—turnover can fit in this context.

After all, as you become a more effective manager, you should naturally see employee dissatisfaction decrease and employee performance increase.

Both a decrease in employee dissatisfaction and an increase in employee performance are obviously good for your bottom line.

77

Similarly, improving workplace culture can increase productivity, engagement, and as a result, profits.

So why is my focus still on turnover? Quite simply because turnover is one of the places you might be costing your business the most money.

Turnover is only very, very rarely a good thing for an organization. If you have someone that is actively holding back your organization (such as a bully that diminishes other employees' engagement and productivity) or even sabotaging the business, then yes, getting them to move and cutting ties is probably what's best for the business.

In almost every other case, though, firing someone or seeing them quit is something you should, as a manager, want to avoid.

Let's look at some of the reasons why turnover should be avoided.

Turnover:
- ***Is expensive.***
- ***Is time-consuming.***
- ***Sets everyone back.***
- ***Affects every employee.***
- ***Hinders growth.***

All of those things are bad—and turnover may have other less obvious implications as well.

As a manager, it is your job to get the most out of your people. What does it say about your own work when you regularly have to fire someone, especially if you were also the person that interviewed and hired them?

Turnover reflects poorly on you as a manager and on your organizational culture. As a manager, it is your job to get the most out of your people. What does it say about your own work when you regularly have to fire someone, especially if you were also the person that interviewed and hired them? What does it say about your work as a manager if people decide to quit rather than work for you?

No matter how you look at turnover, it is rarely good for your business.

Turnover Is Expensive

Numbers vary widely, depending on the source or the study cited, but consider this: Some estimates note that replacing an employee may cost one-and-a-half times their annual salary by the time you factor in all of the expenses that go into finding a replacement, training that replacement, and the knowledge base that is lost when someone leaves.

Some estimates note that replacing an employee may cost one-and-a-half times their annual salary by the time you factor in all of the expenses that go into finding a replacement, training that replacement, and the knowledge base that is lost when someone leaves.

Even if you are looking at low-wage, low-skill (traditionally high-turnover) sorts of positions, simply accounting for the time and cost included in advertising an open position, sorting through applications, interviewing those applicants that make the cut, and then training the new hire is at the very least a cost of several thousand dollars if not significantly more.

Whatever numbers you choose to use...turnover is expensive. The time it takes to replace someone costs more money because it is time you cannot put toward other needs of the business. Similarly, the lack of productive workflow in that position, until you find and train a capable new hire, also hurts your bottom-line. Even turnover in a low-wage position— even turnover in a minimum-wage position—will cost you something.

These opportunity costs associated with turnover can be reduced through better hiring, onboarding, and management processes.

Turnover Is Time-Consuming

But beyond the dollars and cents of turnover, let's think about the time it costs you as a manager. Each time you fire someone or otherwise need to replace someone, you need to write the want ad, post the want ad (likely in multiple places to ensure you actually get responses), review the responses (which, depending on the economic climate in which you are posting the opening, could be like grasping at straws, looking for a needle in a haystack, or anywhere in between), begin the interview process, and then eventually onboard the new employee.

Turn over more than a single employee each year and suddenly a huge chunk of your time gets taken up with hiring to maintain rather than actually working on or growing the business.

That makes it difficult to hold the bottom line steady, much less focus on growing.

Turnover Sets Everyone Back

And that doesn't even take into account the strain that being undermanned puts on your staff. I know that if you have a great crew, they likely step up big time when you are short-staffed. Everyone on the team pulls together to get jobs done, and if your employees are anything like most of mine, they take enough pride in their work to ensure that most customers or clients have no idea the shop was or is short-handed. I know some managers are tempted to think in these situations that their shop is getting by just fine, so maybe they don't even need to fill the now-open position.

And okay, maybe sometimes that is the case. More often than not, though, this line of thinking fails to take into account both how much harder everyone is working to pick up the slack (risking burnout, customer satisfaction, or worse, such as injury on the job) and how individuals may not be able to do their normal job duties because they are instead busy filling the vacated position's roles.

Turnover Affects Every Employee

When people step up when short-handed, that's a good sign of a positive workplace culture. Be careful, though: It isn't sustainable and can do real damage to your workplace morale.

When the people on your team step up and take care of business even when significantly short-handed, that's a good sign of a positive workplace culture, where employees take pride in their work and come together to pick up and take on the tasks normally covered by the vacated position. But that isn't sustainable and can do real damage to your workplace morale.

Additionally, putting your business in that position means you're all just getting by, rather than looking at ways the business can improve and grow. That can lead to stagnation, lowered employee engagement and satisfaction, and in time, customers and clients will start to notice the difference between a fully-staffed shop running at 100% and one which is short-staffed and just trying to get by.

Turnover Hinders Growth

It's awesome that the culture of your organization is such that everyone came together in a time of need, but an empty position has a very real effect on the organization. You may be able to temporarily get the job done, but you will not be able to continue growing the business.

Let's use a concrete example to help make this clear. Think about what happens when an employee is just out for a few days, such as when a tech is absent for a day or two with the flu. How much production is lost? What does this do to the schedule? Even when you expect an absence, such as when vacations are scheduled, too rarely do we plan ahead to ensure everything gets done and done well. The loss in production when someone is out, the increased stress of being short-staffed and the customer challenges that are sometimes created when you are understaffed cannot be undone. You cannot get lost production time, and its associated revenue back. When the time is gone, the time is gone.

Turnover in a position(s) can cause a longer-term loss, lack of growth, or increased stress level than any organization wants or needs for a sustainable future. Turnover creates a more consistent loss that is rarely noticed until year end when this year's

83

numbers are compared to last year's. Even worse, if turnover has been consistent over the years, you might never recognize the potential earnings you are losing.

Learning to manage your people and organization to reduce turnover rates is critical to business growth, no matter how big or small a business you may currently be—or how big you hope to become.

Learning to manage your people and organization to reduce turnover rates is critical to business growth.

Similarly, there is always a difference between being busy and being productive. When you have too few employees to get the job done, the business itself feels busier, sure—but it is not growing, and may actually be slipping backwards. Feeling busy as a human is different than the business being busy. If you're constantly dealing with the turnover, you cannot be busy doing what it takes to grow the business. Sure, some turnover is going to be normal—especially with those entry-level, low-wage positions—but you need to have as little turnover as possible so you can focus on making the business better and helping it (and your employees) grow.

Too many service organizations have too much turnover, and worse yet, don't realize what it is doing to their daily operations.

Hopefully by now, though, you are starting to see just how high the cost of turnover may be.

Chapter 8: Operating in the Gray Area

When you do need to fire an employee, you usually know pretty early on. Perhaps you've tried interventions, scaffolding skills (think of scaffolding as a way of helping your employees build stepping stone skills; if this is something you're interested in, it's well worth doing your research to find scaffolding approaches that might work for you), or other strategies to help this struggling employee fit into the culture and workspace in a way that can benefit everyone involved and it's still clear that this just isn't going to work. Plenty of low-skill, low-pay employees are fired within the first few weeks when it becomes clear that it just isn't a good fit. Still, though, it should be your goal to rarely need to fire even these employees, because ideally you'd learn over time what to ask in interviews and would get better at finding workers more likely to stick, as well as—as your coaching skills improve—get better at helping find ways to make employees fit even if they traditionally might not.

As a result, though, most shop employees tend to stick in a gray area when it comes to skills and experience.

If you think of your own shop, I'd imagine most of your employees have likely been with you for a little while at least. It's pretty rare, though, that you get to keep employees for fifteen or twenty years. Those sort of employees—provided they're fully engaged and invested in the culture and work, as opposed to burnt out and just hanging on because the job is something they know how to do well enough—can be a dream to work with in your shop because they've been around long enough that they have a large institutional knowledge base. Rarely do problems stump these sorts of employees, because they've seen it all before—or something similar enough anyway that they have strategies for solving any problem that might come up.

These employees (and employees like them) can also be great at mentoring new hires, showing them the ropes and introducing them to the organizational culture, as well as of great assistance to you when you need feedback on your managing and help to get employee buy-in.

As we all know, though, those sort of long-term employees are rare. Instead, most employees fall in a sort of a gray area, where they're no longer fresh hires that need supervision at every step or need their hand held, but nor are they the completely autonomous veterans with their institutional knowledge of how things work such that they can simply get the work done as it needs to be done.

Gray area employees:

- *Are not fresh hires or rookies.*
- *But don't have the skills or experience to be quite autonomous, either.*
- *Consequently, can be the most difficult to manage.*

And this gray area is where management can be most difficult. For these employees, you need to learn to recognize when and where close, direct supervision is needed and where autonomy is warranted. You need to recognize when to push and when to pull, and you need to determine how best to motivate and reward your employees while also continuing to challenge them—but without challenging them beyond what they are capable of withstanding. It can be a very fine line, and many managers struggle with finding the right balance. But finding and maintaining that balance is the difference between a healthy, growing organization and one that struggles along, operating at barely more than day-to-day.

To fully realize any organization's potential, owners and managers must learn and develop the skills required to manage both people and processes while also helping a positive organizational culture develop and thrive.

This is, of course, exacerbated by the fact that most of us have little to no management training. Instead, most of us who are now running shops are doing so because we worked our way up the ladder or worked under someone else before starting out on our own. A word of caution here. Although I often make the case that we fire some employees too quickly, rather than coaching them, developing them, or finding a more suitable position for them, there is a big difference between keeping someone on because you believe they'll fit, and keeping someone on because you're afraid of not being able to replace them.

I see many organizations handicapped by a fear of not finding someone as good or better. This is also a form of working in a gray area. Sometimes it is necessary to recognize that you cannot manage from a position of fear. A leap of faith is necessary sometimes. I can say that virtually every time I've seen an employee let go, the next employee to answer the want ad had more knowledge, better attitude, and higher levels of customer satisfaction or management skill.

Never manage in fear. Have faith that all things are meant to be, and manage based on solid principles. That next, better, person will show up.

Remember, managing is not like diagnosing, repairing, or building something. There are not always easy, obvious answers when it comes to managing. This is the gray area. It takes a certain amount of faith that the answers, and people, will come with time and effort. Time will be a great teacher, but you must put in the work and effort, even when you feel like you don't know exactly what to do, or if your solution will work. It is far better, in my opinion, to try something, monitor it's progress, make course adjustments, and see it fail, than it is to do nothing until you are absolutely certain. There are few absolutes in managing, and a lot of gray.

In the next chapter, let's look a bit at the difference between managing people and cultural systems, such as running a business, and managing technical problems, which is where most of us excel.

Chapter 9: Core Business Expectations

Setting expectations is one of the basics of management we mentioned in Chapter 4. In this chapter and the next, we take a deeper look at what expectations you might set such that organizational culture goals are met, and what you can do when those expectations are not met consistently. I would suggest that having high expectations is always far better than having average expectations.

Those organizations that perform at a high level do so for a reason. There is an underlying commitment to achieving high expectations. Don't worry about setting expectations high and then being disappointed. Instead, set them high—and then continue to get better at managing and coaching.

What do you expect as an automotive repair shop? There is likely some common expectation—or even a set of expectations—that you hold. It could be that employees show up on time or produce quality work above all else. Maybe it's that the customer always comes first, or that all processes are adhered to by the letter. Often one or more of these expectations can form your core organizational philosophy (something we'll address more in Chapter 12), but at the very least, these can be your core business expectations.

Those core business expectations should readily translate into the service customers get as well, whether that philosophy is posted on a wall or not. Those expectations—and the core organizational philosophy, which we'll again discuss more in Chapter 12—should permeate your culture and your processes, and as a result, should even be clear to your customers.

Remember that when translating core business expectations to employees, you must do at least two things for each employee:

1. Clearly explain the expectation including examples.
2. Describe, or show (this is best), what the expectation, when successfully met, would look like to the employee and everyone else.

Common core business expectations include:

- *Timeliness*
- *Quality*
- *Production*
- *Adherence to processes*
- *Customers first*

Let's spend a little time on each of these most common core business expectations.

Timeliness

Timeliness, as I define it, could apply in a number of scenarios. It might mean when an employee arrives at work or returns from a break. It could also apply to when a customer is promised their vehicle back. Timeliness essentially means this: Is a given time deadline or goal being met?

As a manager, when it comes to timeliness, there are two big questions to consider. First, is your expectation reasonable? For most managers, timeliness certainly is a reasonable expectation. Second, can you guarantee the expectation will be met? No, probably not. There will always be some employees that are late at least occasionally, just as there will always be at least some work that is delayed by delivery schedules or other extenuating factors.

But that hardly means you shouldn't strive for timeliness just the same.

Make it an organizational expectation that employees are ready to work at a given time.

Instead, make it an organizational expectation that employees are ready to work at a given time, such as 7:30 am if the shop opens at 8, or 8:30 am if the shop opens at 9 am, etc, and then be clear in communicating your expectations, coach your employees up as needed, and adapt your processes as applicable.

When thinking about organizational expectations it is always a good practice to consider if this expectation is reasonable given resource levels, training, precedent, and communication. When it comes to timeliness, you might ask if it is reasonable to expect employees to be ready to work at, and until a given time, if it is reasonable to expect vehicle promised times to be held given your production schedule, and other related questions. You won't always be able to ensure timeliness, but that doesn't mean you cannot or should not set the expectation of timeliness and build a system that holds people accountable.

Quality

When it comes to quality, there are again two questions to consider:

- ***Is it reasonable?***
- ***What does the expectation of quality look like?***

96

First off, expecting quality work should definitely be thought of as a reasonable expectation; without quality, you have no business!

If you do not have a quality product, you will soon have no customers.

As for what that expectation of quality looks like, that will depend on your shop and your managerial standards and processes. A definite best practice to keep in mind when it comes to setting expectations is to describe what the expectation looks like when it is accomplished. In the case of quality maybe we measure it in terms of comebacks, vehicle cleanliness, keeping promised times, always test driving, getting the vehicle fixed right the first time, and so forth. We consider each expectation both in terms of whether or not it is reasonable and what does that expectation of quality look like? How will the customer know they have been provided with quality? These three aspects of the quality expectation will eventually relate to holding employees accountable to the expectation.

See the book Service Management Made Simple for an example of what a Quality Control Process looks like.

Production

Similarly, we have to consider if our expectations for production are reasonable and what those expectations might look like.

Can you expect certain production levels? Maybe. I certainly do with the shops I work with. What this expectation looks like for you, though, will vary widely depending on your managerial style, what you believe is possible, your employees' expertise and skills, and a million other factors. Skill, experience, work conditions, and much more should all factor into your expectations and how you communicate those expectations, but once we have accounted for those factors, we can likely have an overall average production expectation no matter who we have working for us.

Setting production expectations:

- ***Ensure they are reasonable.***
- ***Determine what success looks like so that you know if you are meeting the expectation.***
- ***Determine how you will hold employees accountable to those expectations.***

What does this expectation look like when it is being met? You might have baselines that include hours of productivity for your technicians, daily repair order goals for your service advisors, or a baseline number of follow-up phone calls per week for your organizational support. Those are some of the baselines I use, though yours may vary. In any case, though, a production expectation, for the shop or the service counter, usually has some sort of metric with it. Remember what the management guru Peter Drucker always said: What gets measured, gets changed.

Considering how reasonable the expectation is will be the first step in setting one, what it looks like when met is an important second step, and then thirdly, the ability to measure it is crucial to accountability. Toward that end, work with SMART goals.

SMART goals are:
- **Specific**
- **Measurable**
- **Attainable**
- **Realistic**
- **Time-bound**

Try to stick with SMART goals: Goals that are specific, measurable, attainable, realistic, and time-bound. I won't elaborate any more on SMART goals as a quick Google search will provide you with enough opinion on using, or not using, them to satisfy any boredom you may be experiencing. Suffice it to say that I believe this format is a great way to quickly ensure your expectations and goals are going to be met.

Adherence To Processes

As with each of these other common core business expectations, there are two questions to consider:
- Is being required to adhere to process reasonable?
- What does adhering to process look like?

As a general rule, I certainly think that expecting employees to adhere to your organizational processes is reasonable. Here comes that gray area, however. Does adhering to process mean there will never be instances in which an employee should do things in a different way? No, of course not, but if the expectation is that processes are followed unless there are explicit reasons to do things differently, then an expectation has been clearly communicated and everyone can start from the same page.

But what does that expectation look like for you and your shop? That can vary quite a bit from shop to shop. After all, does this mean following the process to the letter each and every single time, or does it mean generally following the process? What are the parameters of the expectation, and how are they clearly communicated?

This is again a place where your natural managerial style, organizational culture, and employee know-how will likely all factor in. In gray areas like this, I often give the advice to let employees know what you want the end result to be, and let them get there on their own. Organizational situations where every move is dictated by process tend to become more self-limiting than anyone intended. If you've hired well, on-boarded well, and keep to your review process, then you are likely to have employees that can find their own way to the desired result.

Additionally relevant is the effectiveness of each of your processes. If a process is flawed, or only works most of the time, we are setting ourselves up for at least some failure. Likewise, if a process is perfect but our employees don't have the requisite skills to perfectly follow that process, we are also setting ourselves up for failure.

As a result, both designing good processes and ensuring the expectations of those processes is met by each and every employee can be tremendously difficult even for experienced managers, much less for those managers just getting their feet underneath themselves.

Know that this is one of those places where you will likely need quite a bit of trial and error. Be upfront with your employees and clearly communicate that you are working with them to find what works. Changes will be needed, and may even be frequent (at least at first), but if those changes are made with employee input, that will help tremendously, especially if they know why the changes are being made. Know, too, that you will also need to be flexible and adaptable as you search for what will work best. You are not trying to take individuality out of the organization, but instead trying to create some consistency in how things are done.

As a manager, you can set yourself up for success by including employees in setting the expectation(s), measuring the accomplishment of the expectation, and holding each other accountable to the process. Sometimes having the group develop the expectation is enough to move things in the consistent forward direction you are looking for. And again, use SMART goals as you work toward developing your perfect and preferred processes.

Customers First

Customer-first business expectations can similarly be difficult, both in setting the expectations and ensuring a culture that is equipped to handle and exceed those expectations.

What does this look like for you as a manager? While it varies a bit from shop to shop, most customer-first businesses have a few core tenets.

Customer-first expectations:

- *Customers can easily book service appointments.*
- *Customers know their vehicle will be respected and Fixed Right the First Time.*

- ***The organization will do whatever it takes to provide high levels of customer convenience.***

Now, those are admittedly lofty standards. Not every shop has the staff or space to readily accommodate those expectations. For every manager that wishes to be a "customers first" manager or owner, however, there are a few things to keep in mind as you set expectations.

First, be sure to clearly describe what your vision of this looks like both to your employees and your customers. Your idea of customer-first service may be different than my idea of customer-first service, which may, in turn, be very different than various employees' or customers' expectations. This is an example of where communication of the expectation becomes incredibly important. This is about an organizational expectation, not an individual employee's expectation.

Customer-first expectations can be different from generation to generation and from person to person and, truthfully, are often very intrinsically connected to each individual's own personal experience. As a result, coming to an accepted and collective agreement as to what this expectation looks like can be incredibly difficult without specific and clear communication. Having some customer data available, such as survey or focus group responses, can help provide a customer perspective during these conversations.

Even then, defining, describing, and measuring this expectation will take some time. That said, being a customer-first business may well become a core organizational philosophy when you're ready to develop your core philosophy, so taking the time to clearly define both the expectation and the processes that help fulfill the expectation can and should be time well-spent.

A SMART Goal Example

With each and every single one of these core business expectations—or any other core business expectations you may have in their place—setting and adjusting SMART goals can be tremendously helpful.

SMART goals are specific, measurable, attainable, realistic, and time-bound.

SMART goals are specific, measurable, attainable, realistic, and time-bound, so if you are looking at developing a customer-first service expectation, for instance, you might have a SMART goal that looks something like this:

- Within the next year, our shop efficiency will be such that 85% of customers are able to book an appointment for work within a week of their call-in date or original service visit.

- 90% of brake jobs will be completed within a 3-hour service window by the end of the calendar year.

Both of these goals are specific, measurable, attainable, realistic, and time-bound, or could be if your shop was in a position to make such goals. What is realistic and attainable for one shop, after all, may be a dream for another. Be realistic in setting your goals and be willing to revise as needed with feedback from stakeholders such as department heads, employees, and trusted customers.

SMART goals can also be a great part of creating your organizational culture, as well, whether team-wide or simply as part of individual employees' annual performance reviews. You can connect SMART goals to employees you are coaching or mentoring, and you can use them to set and effectively communicate clear expectations.

Chapter 10: Willingness to Adapt and Model

Related to setting your core business expectations, accept—and remind yourself as often as needed—that everyone is different. You cannot take a one-size-fits-all approach to your team, just as you cannot with customers, because the same strategies will not work for every single employee. You can have core business expectations that you expect every employee to embrace, but you cannot reasonably expect that it will look exactly the same from every employee every single time—because that simply isn't how people work.

You can and cannot expect:

- *Cannot expect everyone to do things exactly like you.*

- *Can expect some individual deviation.*
- *Can expect some lack of clarity and meaning.*

As an owner or manager, you have to be careful sometimes when setting expectations. Never forget that nobody will ever do things exactly like you would—and that's okay! When we talk about setting expectations, we are not talking about everyone doing things the exact same way. We are talking about describing a result and letting individuals find their way to that result in their own way, within some guidelines. As a manager, you can expect people to do things their own way, be confused about what you meant, and to, as often as not, not do it the way you intended they do it.

Don't be confused about what that means. Just because people don't necessarily do things the way you meant, that doesn't mean they are fighting the system, are incompetent, or anything else. It just means maybe the communication wasn't what it needed to be, you may have to do some coaching, or the person has some barrier to understanding what precisely it was that you were looking for. If you are continually frustrated with setting expectations, take the time to take a step back and think objectively about what that may be. It may be that you are, in fact, the problem.

If you are continually frustrated with setting expectations, take the time to take a step back

and think objectively about what that may be. It may be that you are, in fact, the problem.

To determine whether or not that may be the case, review the problem expectation for reasonableness (based on objective things such as resources available, the skill level of the employees struggling with the expectation, and so forth—not whether YOU think it is a reasonable expectation), whether it is a measurable expectation or not, and how the expectation has been communicated. If you think all of these pieces are in place and things are still not working out, it's likely time to bring everyone together and, as a group, set a new expectation to accomplish what you need. Describe the end result and ask what the process expectation is that will take the organization to that result looks like. It may help to return to the idea of SMART goals here to provide some clarity.

Troubleshooting Expectations

To help troubleshoot, it may help to revisit how you set expectations as well.

When setting your expectations,

- **Be as specific as possible.**
- **Give examples of success.**
- **Be inclusive.**

Never forget that when setting expectations to be as specific as possible, give examples of what success looks like, and whenever possible, be inclusive.

Inclusivity is a not-so-secret management tool that can work some real magic, especially as it comes with built-in accountability and often reduces the amount of time managing takes.

Including others in a decision is not always easy for type-A personalities that may have been rockstar technicians in their past, but it is a great management tool! Inclusivity comes with built-in accountability and often reduces the amount of time managing takes because it naturally creates investment and engagement among those who feel like they had a voice at the table.

Managing Expectations

Managing expectations:

- *Some expectations are simple, intuitive, and relatively easy.*
- *Others are more complex and require more skill to set and hold employees accountable.*
- *It's always best if expectations are documented.*

Setting and clearly communicating expectations is one thing. Managing them—and managing employees—is much more difficult.

Some expectations—like show up on time for work—can be simple, intuitive, and as a result, relatively easy. It's pretty well understood that a basic expectation of any job is showing up for work on time. Other expectations, such as don't be rude to customers, are likewise straightforward.

One such straightforward expectation: Every organization should require employees to punch in and out of work and breaks using a timeclock or timeclock software.

But that's hardly the case with every expectation, including some of the expectations that may prove to be core business expectations.

Some expectations will be much more complex (such as an organizational diagnostic flow to ensure all diagnostic time is accounted for, for instance) and as such, will require much more work on your part. You will need to learn to coach, mentor, and listen well. (something we'll talk about in greater depth in Chapter 17). You will need to measure and monitor employees' success. Managing employees working toward meeting a given requirement may require more handholding—in some cases, significantly more handholding than you might be comfortable with.

And that's okay! Part of the growing process as both a manager and an organization is working through difficult times, including embracing hard transitions. That, of course, doesn't mean that you shouldn't be willing to recognize when your organization isn't ready for a change, or when you need a better approach for introducing a change, but it does mean you should be ready for difficulties in managing expectations.

Documenting expectations is a great accountability tool.

There are ways you can make these changes a little easier for you and for your employees that might struggle with them, however. If you can document expectations, for instance, it can be a great accountability tool. You won't have to document every expectation, but for the major ones, you will definitely want documentation.

Let's look at a few examples.

Timeliness can be a difficult expectation to manage for some teams. Timeliness can and should be measured. If I'm clocking in and out for the day (including breaks), it's really hard for me to argue whether or not I'm being timely. This is an expectation that is easy to set from the first day of hire. If you have not traditionally required employees to clock in and out, now is the time to start! If you are new to setting expectations and managing them, this is also a great one to start with. It is an easy expectation to understand, easy to measure (especially if you get yourself some web-based software to track clock-in and clock-out times), and a good expectation with which to practice managing. Continuing to use timeliness as our example, be specific about setting the expectation.

Try using specific language, like the example phrases below:

- *As an employee, we expect you to be ready to work—in uniform, ready to perform your duties—by 8 am.*
- *The reason we expect this is that we pride ourselves on customer service, and customers will be waiting at 8 am.*
- *Customers expect us to be open and ready to work at 8 am when we promised. We expect you to be ready, too.*

Use these word tracks as an example of how you might describe the expectation. I often use the analogy of getting kids on a school bus. The bus will show up roughly the same time each day (as will the start of work). If you don't care about breakfast, sleep in your clothes, and never brush your teeth, well, then, you can get up two minutes before the bus arrives and make it on time. If you like to shower, eat pancakes, and do your hair, you'll need to get up an appropriate amount of time before the bus arrives. In either case, the bus will be there, and in either case, work starts the same time every day, so be ready, no matter what you need to do to get ready.

But let's be honest with each other. There will still be employees that don't meet the expectation, of course. But this gives the framework in which to deal with that problem as it arises. Now if an employee misses the expectation, we have a framework in which to manage that behavior and hold them accountable. Most of the time, a discussion is enough.

When an expectation isn't met, consider this example process:

- *Strike 1: Mention the miss.*
- *Strike 2: Longer conversation.*
- *Strike 3: Formal sit down.*
- *Strike 4: Written notice.*
- *Strike 5: Sent home without pay.*
- *Strike 6: Termination.*

Continuing to use timeliness as our example here, these are the steps I use to try and correct the problem behavior. I'll admit that I tend to be more patient than some are. The first miss, I mention the miss. The second miss I have a slightly longer conversation about missing the mark. The third time something happens we have a formal sit-down discussion. If for some reason it happens a fourth time, the employee gets a written notice. The fifth time, I'll send the employee home without pay for the day. After that, the employee will likely be asked to find other employment. Of course, this isn't always so cut-and-dry; there are sometimes other circumstances that will dictate how you handle things. Usually, by the time we get to a fifth offense, though, the employee sees on their own that it's time to move on.

You may choose to be less lenient than I am, and that's fine. You'll have to find what works for you. Remember, you're always looking for that sweet spot between firing an employee too quickly, and keeping an underperforming employee too long.

Let's look at managing a process expectation because that can be much more difficult to manage than a simple expectation like timeliness.

Another example: Processes

- *Not every process is perfect.*
- *Not every process works in every situation or every time.*
- *Processes may have individual components as well, and each individual may follow a process slightly differently.*

Managing a process expectation can be very different than managing something like an easily-measured timeliness expectation. Not every process is perfect. If nothing else, processes can have many variables in how things happen each day or each transaction. If you feel a process expectation is not being met, you may need to examine the expectation and how you presented it.

For instance, were you specific enough? Is it the entire process that is not working or simply a part of the process? If a part of the process seems to be the problem, which part? Can we have a separate expectation for just this part?

Troubleshoot problem expectations piece-by-piece and you may have better luck finding solutions.

Example Process: Service Counter Workflow

Let's look at an example process, like your service counter workflow. Your processes may be slightly different, but in general, there's a pattern to everyone's service counter process:

- Customer greeting.
- Information acquisition (using certain forms).
- RO write-up.
- Dispatch to a technician.
- Courtesy inspection conducted.
- Whatever steps might need to come next, workflow dependent.

Here is a process that might have some challenges. For the sake of argument, let's say that the process works for the most part. Our observations each morning show that the customers are being greeted well, we're gathering information, the ROs are written up consistently (for the most part, anyway), and the dispatch process is working just fine. We don't, however, seem to be completing courtesy inspections very well. An audit of weekly ROs shows that fewer than half of the ROs have had inspections conducted, and of those inspections, many of them were not filled out very well. Those courtesy inspections that were conducted resulted in very few upsells. In this case, the process expectation is mostly being met—yet a very important part of the process is failing.

The problem? Courtesy inspections are not very good.

- Rarely is there enough information to sell anything.
- The notes included are of poor quality.
- Too few inspections are actually being completed.

In this particular case, doing a thorough review of the courtesy inspections that were being done revealed that the incomplete information included on the courtesy inspection forms was proving to be a barrier to the advisors upselling potential work. The technician notes were frequently poor, there were few included pictures, and rarely any measurements—all of which made upselling far more difficult.

A few example strategies we could have taken:

- *"Because I said so."*

- *Firing the problem employee.*
- *Investing more money in technology.*
- *Giving up and going back to the old approach.*
- *Examining the root problem.*

There are a number of ways you can handle this situation. Often our natural inclination is to simply lean on the age-old approach: Do it because I said so.

Adding a touch of grumpiness to this if it doesn't work the first time is usually the next approach taken. Sometimes yelling, screaming, and threatening in an emergency shop meeting will be the final approach before we resign ourselves. Well, it's your money is what resignation, in this case, might look like, unfortunately.

Other approaches including firing the individual deemed not doing their job, investing in more technology believing there must be a better way, or just giving up and going back to business as usual. While each of these approaches may sometimes be warranted, they are hardly ideal, for multiple reasons.

Firing people costs money and limits continuity as well as decreases shop morale. Investing more money in technology obviously costs money—and may or may not fix the problem. Giving up and going back to business as usual won't help us improve a thing.

Instead, we may need to look deeper if we want to find a real solution. What's the root problem? Maybe there's something we just aren't seeing. Yes, it should be simple and may appear to be a simple process, but there still could be something we're missing. And, as often as not, that's exactly what is happening. Let me explain.

Asking our employees for feedback, rather than telling them what they are doing wrong, can do wonders. Be an active listener, be observant, and see what those involved in the process—in this example case, our service counter workflow and courtesy inspections—have to say about the process. Including employees in the diagnosis and solution in a real and truly inclusive way can work some real magic sometimes!

Often the core problem is not what we think it is.

We may think it's trouble employees or a technology issue, but often it's something entirely different that we aren't seeing because we aren't asking the right questions.

A good manager looks past what's on the surface— and a great manager asks questions that get to what the real problem might be. Learning to ask 'why' at least five times is a great tool to use when doing root cause analysis. This was a technique taught me by my mentors during my time working for Toyota. Try it!

You'll be amazed at what detail it will drill down to, and what it uncovers for you.

Learning to ask 'why' at least five times is a great tool to use when doing root cause analysis.

As smart as we think we are, sometimes the problem is not what we think it is. Learn to ask yourself if there's something you are missing. Is there something else that I'm not seeing? Include your employees in the diagnosis—the front-line users often have a very different take on things. This isn't to say that they have the answers, or that what they perceive is always correct, but it is all part of the resolution and should be a part of your problem-solving strategy.

What did this look like in a client's shop?

When we had problems with the service counter workflow and courtesy inspections, we did exactly what I'm recommending you do:

- We asked service advisors.
- We asked technicians.
- We took their feedback and looked at the form.
- The real root issue? The form.
- Fixing the form was the real solution we needed.

When we had issues with our service counter workflow and the courtesy inspections not leading to enough upsells, we tried a few things before realizing we weren't getting the feedback we needed from employees.

As a result, we one day scheduled a sit-down meeting with groups of employees to try and really get to the root issues.

The challenge was exactly what we've described previously: Too few inspections were being done, and those that were done were incomplete. As a result, the courtesy inspections weren't leading to upsells.

Each group of employees—both the service advisors and the technicians—wanted to blame the other group. When we kept asking questions, though, we got to the real issue; when everyone was ready to stop pointing fingers, they could identify the true culprit and come to an agreement that the inspection form was the real issue, as it simply didn't work for anyone involved.

Not only was there not enough room on the paper form to leave appropriately detailed notes, but the form as currently constructed also requested information on systems and components that didn't necessarily fit the vehicles being inspected. As a result, the technicians found the form to be a waste of time and consequently didn't fill it out very well. Without adequate notes, the service advisors could not sell anything.

121

The technicians "pencil whipping" the form was a result of so many irrelevant lines of components and systems. At the same time, a few technicians were cherry picking the form to make some money, but still not really understanding the real purpose of a free courtesy inspection nor how to really make the process work for everyone involved.

As you can imagine, all in all, it was a recipe for disaster.

Once we got all the real root issue information to the forefront, however, it was much easier to find potential solutions.

Our resolution suggestions looked something like this:

- ***Meet with advisors to discuss too few inspections, how to work with the notes they have, and what information to additionally ask for from the techs.***
- ***Meet with techs to do the same.***
- ***Ask each group for their solutions and then workshop ways to use those that are most applicable.***
- ***As we make the modifications, keep meeting with both groups—ideally together—and get confirmation that the changes are really what they wanted.***

By working with both groups and continually affirming that we had a correct understanding of what changes they needed for the process to be effective, we were able to make the process work for everyone involved.

Additionally, because we had gotten so much input everyone felt engaged, valued, and was more willing to embrace the changes.

By asking each side of the relationship for their input and their proposed solutions, we were able to adapt the form in ways that worked for everyone. Longer-term, the changes increased both the number of inspections performed and the quality of the inspections, which in turn led to increases in revenue, gross profit, and customer satisfaction.

As often as not, managing is about problem solving—really in that way, it's no different than diagnosing and repairing vehicles. Managers simply problem solve with people and processes rather than mechanical contraptions.

Chapter 11: Starting with Baby Steps

Baby steps:

- *Most things with people are not solved quickly or easily.*
- *Small steps are very often a much better choice toward resolution.*
- *Take time and patience, and reflect that growth can be hard.*

When you are trying to solve problems with people and processes, you will often find that resolution does not come quickly or easily. Sometimes the hold-up is simply a matter of the solution overwhelming the individual (or individuals) that require the change. In that case, baby steps are often required; it's better to make small progressive change than running up against a wall of resistance. Butting your head against a wall doesn't feel good or result in change; small steps forward, however, do both.

Giving employees a series of small wins can:

- *Make your point.*
- *Get employees more engaged and invested in change.*
- *Show steady improvement.*

Change does not come easily to most of us. The same is often true for our employees. Using a patient approach, recognizing that this can be hard for individuals affected, and accepting that it will take the time it takes can make embracing change a little easier for everyone involved.

Using Targets And Goals

We talked a bit about SMART goals in previous chapters, and I want you to circle back to them because it's easy to underestimate just how incredibly effective they can be as a way of using baby steps to help employees embrace change.

A few guidelines for setting targets and goals:

- *Setting targets can help develop milestones toward larger goals.*
- *Breaking up larger goals into smaller pieces makes them more achievable in a*

shorter time as well as makes them less daunting.
- *Smaller target goals that are attainable can help employees move forward, one baby step at a time.*
- *SMART goals are specific, measurable, attainable, realistic, and time-bound.*
- *Embrace positivity and celebrate each baby step achievement.*

Using these SMART goals as baby steps to help employees reach intermediate goals on their way to your larger target goal is and can be a form of coaching (which we'll address further in Chapter 17), especially when there are easy metrics involved. Often, just giving an employee a target can result in the improvement we are looking for in them and their behavior. This is especially true if, as they achieve intermediate target goals, they start to become more invested and engaged in the process.

That's just one of the many reasons it's important that when we set those intermediate target goals we need to make sure that they are attainable. We don't want to make them so attainable that we are inadvertently humiliating or demeaning our employees (or being condescending; these are, after all, capable human beings we are talking about here), but we also don't want to make them so challenging as to make them impossible.

*The best managers are like firm
but effective teachers.*

The best managers are like firm but effective teachers: They set their intermediate target goals in that range that challenges their employees but also supports them, goals which are certainly attainable but not insultingly so.

After all, there's no point in using intermediate target goals as baby steps toward your larger goal if your employees either feel looked down on or like they are being asked to do something impossible.

Keep Idiosyncratic People In Mind

Remember the lessons of Chapter 5 as you set your baby step intermediate target goals. People can be difficult and unpredictable; people are idiosyncratic.

People:
- *Don't readily embrace change.*
- *Can easily feel overwhelmed.*
- *Will rarely ever think or act the way you think they should.*
- *Are unpredictable and variable.*
- *Need to have those small wins to embrace change.*

Change is difficult. Humans are not really wired to readily accept change. Sometimes we just feel really overwhelmed when faced with making a necessary change in light of all the other duties of the day, week, or month. Employees also don't naturally think like you do—no one does, for that matter—but nor do they need to think like you to do a good job! In fact, sometimes it's better that they don't think like you; after all, they have a different job to do than you. As such, though, they may not feel the need to make certain changes—changes you may know they need to make in order to make the organization better or the shop more efficient and productive, for instance.

So when you are asking your employees to embrace change, be patient, show some small wins with the use of those baby steps and intermediate target goals, and remember the J curve of change. There is always a performance decrease when implementing change. Ride out the rough spots, make modifications as necessary, and you'll eventually gain the performance the change was intended to help you and your organization attain.

About That J Curve...

If you aren't familiar with the J curve theory of change, the J curve refers to this idea that when implementing new change things usually get slightly worse before they get better. That is, performance dips before it improves, like the dip in the letter J.

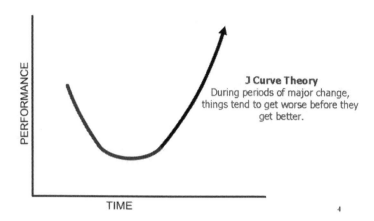

PERFORMANCE

J Curve Theory
During periods of major change,
things tend to get worse before they
get better.

TIME

4

A few pointers:

- *The more complex the process, the more inclusive you'll want to be as you troubleshoot issues, work to increase engagement, and adapt the process to your team.*
- *People feel valued as they are included, and they tend to be as committed to something as they feel valued.*
- *You also need your employees to gradually become better at solving these problems on their own, so coach up their problem-solving skills.*
- *Always document processes, especially those you have trouble with or are trying to revise and improve.*

130

Don't forget the power of inclusivity, either. It really can work magic! Inclusivity makes people feel that they are valued, connects them more closely to the organization (and others in the organization), and builds accountability among team members.

Eventually, you'll need others to solve problems on their own, especially as you'll be busy enough with all the other parts of running the business.

Including everyone in both the diagnosis of challenges and problem resolution teaches them how to problem solve on their own.

Including your employees in both the diagnosis of challenges and problem resolution will also help develop and grow their confidence in themselves and your confidence in them! Using documentation can help flesh out ideas, allow you to better make modifications to existing processes, and provides a ready-made accountability tool.

Additionally, keep in mind that the goal of great managing is to create a team that doesn't need you there to do a great job. You want to work yourself out of a job, and by learning to manage well, you will also be transferring those management skills to others in the organization. This will ultimately create a very strong, sustainable organization. You'll be free to do the important work that only an owner or manager can do while others keep the ship running using the skill set that you helped them to develop.

Keep in mind:

- *Not only are you learning and executing management skills, but you should also be passing those skills along as a teacher and coach.*
- *As others pick up management skills, they can take tasks off your plate, allowing you to focus your time and energy elsewhere.*
- *Exemplifying inclusivity is something you can then have others use in managing the organization as well.*
- *This allows the organization to eventually function on its own without you.*

Chapter 12: Setting a Core Organizational Philosophy

In Chapter 9, we talked about core business expectations. I want to build on that by discussing setting a core organizational philosophy. Your core organizational philosophy should represent everything your organization is all about—what it stands for and what it prioritizes. If built well, a core organizational philosophy can help set the expectations for, and of, every individual in your organization, from yourself to your techs and service advisors, even all the way to any contractors you may work with or interns you may have for the summer, for instance.

Why you need a core organizational philosophy:

- *Having a core organizational philosophy is like a compass for your business.*

- *It provides direction no matter what the question or concern.*
- *When in doubt, employees can lean on this philosophy for guidance.*

A core organizational philosophy is just what it sounds like: It's the guiding principle(s) for everything that happens in your business. As a result, it rests at the center of every decision you or your employees make.

A core organizational philosophy acts as a decision framework when processes or expectations don't cover every eventuality. An organization with a strong core philosophy functions well even when things go awry. If and when questions come about regarding how to handle any given situation, a core philosophy can help answer the dilemma. As a result, if an employee returns to the core organizational philosophy when faced with a difficult situation, they can usually make the right decision without any other guidance—simply by relying on that guiding philosophy.

Let's look at a few examples of core organizational philosophies:

- *Our customers get our best. Always.*
- *At XYZ Automotive we go beyond your expectations, to always deliver a positive customer impact.*

- *We make our customer's automotive service experience easy.*
- *Easy, convenient, transparent.*
- *Only the best. Period.*

Of course, just having a philosophy is not enough; it has to be translated into meaningful action to be effective. A core philosophy can't just be empty sales rhetoric; instead, it needs to guide principles and policies.

When thinking about designing your own organizational philosophy, there are a few guiding principles you should keep in mind. *Keep it simple, understandable, and memorable.* If you can do those three things, you are far more likely to get employee engagement and investment. It will also be far easier to explain and remember.

Your core organizational philosophy should be *Simple, Understandable, and Memorable.*

If you don't have a core philosophy for your organization and want to develop one (and let me be clear, you should; it can—when done well—make managing much easier), be sure to keep it simple, understandable, and memorable.

Your core organizational philosophy is not just a saying or a sales slogan, but should be something that sits at the forefront of every employees' brain, which means it needs to catch. Employees need to be able to quickly think of your organizational philosophy when in doubt as to what to do.

Business history is full of stories where employees did the extraordinary because they leaned on a well-articulated core organizational philosophy.

Business history is full of stories where employees did the extraordinary because they leaned on a well-articulated core organizational philosophy in a time of questions—and let's be honest, that's the kind of business history you want for your organization, too. Wouldn't you rather your organization be the sort that is built to last, where employees are empowered to make big decisions and make them well, and where your business is poised to do extraordinary things? I know I would, and that's why our core organizational philosophy was such a big part of my shop.

Of course, there's one big caveat here, and one that is often lost by managers grasping at strategies rather than fully embracing one: Having a stated philosophy isn't in and of itself enough. You must actually use the philosophy for it to be effective in transforming and elevating your business.

Use your philosophy. Use it well, and use it consistently. Use it when:

- **Setting expectations.**
- **Onboarding new hires.**

- *Holding people accountable.*

When you set expectations, remind the organization that the expectation is in line with the core organizational philosophy. When you hire new employees, introduce them to the core organizational philosophy as a way of introducing them to the organization and helping set the tone for those organizational expectations.

Even better, make your core organizational philosophy a central part of your interviewing and hiring process! Just as importantly, when you need to reprimand or redress or otherwise hold employees accountable, use your core philosophy to help you do so. Simply ask them if the actions taken (or not taken) were in line with the philosophy and you'll have a great way of helping refocus employees on the behaviors you expect to see from them.

When you hire new employees, introduce them to the core organizational philosophy as a way of introducing them to the organization.

So How Do You Determine Your Core Organizational Philosophy?

Start by writing down the first thing that comes to mind. Now, does that encompass the rest of your organizational principles and what you want your business to represent and stand for? Lastly, is there a way to simplify it? If you can simplify it without diluting its power, you need to.

Remember, your core organizational philosophy should be simple, understandable, and memorable.

Next, believe it. Your core organizational philosophy has to be something you and your employees can truly believe in and get behind. If you don't believe it, don't waste your time on it, because your employees will know you don't mean it and they won't invest in it either. Actions speak louder than words, so remember your philosophy has to be something each member of the organization can and will believe in.

Toward that end, you have to use it in every aspect of your management practices. If you can make your organizational philosophy a backbone of everything your company does, and use it to inform every decision you make, your employees will do the same.

Don't create a core organizational philosophy, however, if you don't believe it or if it is hard for employees to believe it. The philosophy must be in line with who and what your organization is. You will use it every day as a guiding principle in your management practices, and the right core organizational philosophy will be used daily by employees—as long as it is constructed well and communicated appropriately.

Steps to building a core organizational philosophy:

- *Write down what first comes to mind.*
- *Revise to ensure it encompasses your organizational principles.*
- *Simplify it as you can without diluting its power.*
- *Believe it.*
- *Utilize it as best you can, incorporating it into every business and managerial decision.*

Chapter 13: Turnover

Some thoughts on turnover:

- *Yes, sometimes people need to be let go.*
- *But what if you could better manage your staff so you turned over half as many people as you do now?*
- *How would reduced turnover limit costs?*
- *How would reduced turnover increase productivity?*
- *Would reduced turnover positively affect employee morale and your organizational culture?*

Turnover can be a dirty word. No one reading this book, I would hope, enjoys laying employees off. It's my goal in this book to help you find strategies so that you'll never need to lay anyone off again. Those strategies include smart hiring, but even more, creating an organizational culture that gets the best out of every single organizational member.

When your people feel supported and pushed forward, are held accountable and trusted to do their work and do it well, turnover becomes less of an issue. And in the coming chapters, we'll look at strategies to help you create those types of organizational culture.

All of that said, an important caveat: Yes, there are occasionally times when you are better off cutting your losses and letting an employee go. Not everyone is cut out for your organization, your culture, or how you prefer to do business.

As I hope you'll realize while we work through this book together, if you make certain changes to your organization, the organizational culture will begin to shift such that employees that don't fit the "new" culture will begin to self-select out of the system, while at the same time the new culture will begin to attract individuals who are better suited to your growth and sustainability goals. When managed well, organizational change will help those already within the organization to adapt, grow, and prosper in ways you've never imagined.

As a result, you shouldn't any longer need to let underperforming employees hold you hostage. Instead, if you take the lessons of this book to heart and implement the changes your organization needs, you should see either (or both!) of the aforementioned changes in your trouble employees: Either they will realize that they don't fit in your organization and self-select themselves out, or they will make the changes necessary in themselves in order to become a contributing member of that culture.

Two keys to limiting turnover and creating a strong organization:

- ***Understanding management principles and how you can best use them.***
- ***Understanding best practices for building the organizational culture you want.***

So here's what I hope you have found so far in this book: An understanding of how to better manage people, both in understanding management principles and in recognizing best practices for building the organizational culture you want.

Toward that end, it helps considerably, however, if you determine several things.

Questions to ask yourself:

- ***What kind of manager are you naturally? (And what are the strengths and weaknesses of that management style, so you can adapt as needed).***

- *What is your current organizational culture?*
- *What are the strengths of that culture?*
- *Where does that culture need to be readdressed and modified to get the most out of your people?*

These are big, business-changing questions. You need to know what kind of manager you naturally are. Until you know this, you cannot recognize the strengths or weaknesses of how you naturally manage, much less adapt as needed by your employees and your business. Similarly, you need to identify your current organizational culture, both to recognize and celebrate its strengths and to address the places where you can make it stronger and more positive. Otherwise, your business will never be able to get the most out of your people. By addressing your organizational culture, however, and becoming a stronger manager, you can help get the most out of your people in helping them learn and grow—while also learning and growing yourself.

Answering these important questions takes both time and effort. All the skills we've discussed up to this point are important skills to develop and concepts to understand if you are to become the best manager you can be. Understanding your own management style will take your learning the next step. I am often suggesting to clients and class participants that much of managing is choosing the words you use. It's one thing to know that expectations, communication, objectivity, and coaching are critical components of managing, but how you go about influencing these things, both instinctually and consciously, will determine your success, or lack thereof.

As I've mentioned previously, most businesses are formed in the image of their founder—for better or worse. If your first instinct is to yell, scream, and berate an employee for not getting the job done, then you will attract employees who are used to high-turnover organizations. This won't be intentional, but you'd be surprised how often like attracts like even in business. Furthermore, this results in an organization that operates on emotions, both positive and negative, and has very little consistency in both quality workmanship or customer experience.

If you are someone who goes pretty easy on employees and shies away from conflict, you are likely to attract employees who are used to taking advantage of managers like you and will use these traits to underperform for long periods of time. These organizations tend to produce low gross profits, have customer bases that are in a constant state of flux, and are generally underperforming.

Understanding that turnover in an organization is not something that will ever be eliminated, but rather something that can be controlled, and understanding the underlying elements of what reduces turnover will help to create an organization with the traits that allow it to be self-sufficient, provide quality workmanship, and have high levels of customer satisfaction.

I am not suggesting that reducing turnover is the key to building a stronger organization, but rather that those attributes that create a strong, sustainable business lend themselves to reduced turnover and increased profits. In my opinion, it is well worth the studying and effort it will take to learn to build and manage a strong organization.

Chapter 14: Management Styles

Let's start this chapter with an understatement: Managing people is never an easy task. Nor is it one you will ever perfect; good management constantly evolves and grows with the lessons of experience and a willingness to change as needed for the good of your business.

Managing people is never an easy task. It is a skill that you will likely never perfect, but instead will learn that it constantly evolves and grows.

If you understand this as a starting point you're well on your way to being a good manager of people and resources. You will also need to recognize that although you may have a dominant style of management, any given style may not work for every situation. You may have to learn a new style(s) and recognize where, and with who, to apply each.

A single management style will not be applicable to all situations. You will need to learn, and utilize, different management styles for different people and situations.

So we'll need to start by helping you learn to recognize your own natural management style. In general, managers work from one of three broad schools of thought or styles.

Styles of management:

- **Autocratic**
- **Democratic**
- **Laissez-Faire**

Let's take a quick look at each school of thought. We're going to keep this brief; a deep dive could literally take us years and at least an M.B.A. if not a Ph.D., and that's not what we're looking for here. We want this to be a guide for you, a manager.

Instead of diving deep, I simply want to help you quickly recognize the type of manager you are so that you can recognize both the strengths and weaknesses of your natural approach to management and adapt as needed to better build a great organizational culture.

Keep in mind, too, that both internal and external factors will influence your natural management style and the management style that might work best in your organization.

Internal factors include:

- ***Organizational priorities and policies.***
- ***Existing corporate culture and management structures.***
- ***Staff skill levels and motivations.***

Internal factors might include organizational priorities and policies, existing corporate culture, staff skill levels and motivations, and even existing management structures, depending on the type of organization in which you work. Broadly put, though, in order to be effective, your managerial style and outlook must fit into the larger organizational culture—including both those policies and procedures already in place and a need to meet organizational objectives.

The less skilled or motivated your people, the greater the oversight they might need. Conversely, the more skilled or motivated your workforce, the more autonomy you may be able to give them.

It's especially important when considering internal factors that your management style account for the skill levels and motivations of those employees working under you. The less skilled or motivated your people, the greater the oversight they might need. Conversely, the more skilled or motivated your

149

workforce, the more autonomy you may be able to give them.

External factors include:

- ***Consumers***
- ***Competitors***
- ***Suppliers***
- ***Economic context***
- ***Laws and regulations***

External factors might include consumers, competitors, suppliers, the general economic context, or even the laws governing your workplace and industry. For instance, a competitor might affect your workforce pool if they are able to pay or offer better working conditions, benefits, or other draws that may make it more difficult for you to gain the best workers. Consumers may dictate what you are able to charge, thus affecting your margins and how you are able to set work hours, etc. The general economic context may help determine the demand for your services, for instance, or what wages workers are willing to accept as fair market value. Regulations governing the workforce or the work you offer may also change, which can result in a need for different certifications or skills. All these factors can contribute to which management styles may be most effective.

But I'm getting ahead of myself. Before you can better identify which places you may need to adapt your management style, you first must understand how you naturally manage.

Let's look more closely at those three management styles I mentioned previously.

Autocratic leaders

- *Tend to be the most controlling and authoritarian.*
- *Are most common in hierarchical organizations.*
- *Work best with employees lower in skill or motivation who need more direction and supervision.*

Of the three management styles, autocratic leaders are the most controlling and authoritarian. In hierarchical organizations, this management style is more common, as roles and tasks are clearly defined and employees are expected to follow these preestablished roles without question. Similarly, employees' ideas or contributions are neither asked for nor encouraged. Communication is primarily (if not extensively) top-down.

I would like to point out that this style of leadership often is the first adopted by new shop owners. Its prominence in the automotive industry often leads new owners to the "do it my way because it works" mentality that then gets ingrained in the organization over time. When this managerial style becomes the

151

dominant type of management, it makes the concept of 'working on the business, rather than in the business' a very difficult transition. This style of management certainly has its place, but the manager must have an awareness of when, and when not, to use it.

Employees that may benefit from an autocratic management style tend toward the less-skilled or lower-motivated end of the spectrum, as they tend to benefit more from the clear direction and supervision.

While clearly defined roles and expectations are an advantage of an autocratic management style, as is lack of potential confusion (given that direction is wholly top-down), there are also clear disadvantages of autocratic management. Because staff input is generally not encouraged (and may even, in fact, be actively discouraged), employees may become dissatisfied with their role in the organization in a way that contributes to an "us vs them" mentality. Not all employees need the high level of supervision most common in autocratic management models, either, and these factors may lead to turnover, low job satisfaction, absenteeism, and other contributors to diminished employee performance.

Varieties of autocratic management include:

- ***Authoritative***
- ***Persuasive***
- ***Paternalistic***

Authoritative

Authoritative managers do not trust their employees. Direct orders are given, and the expectation is that orders will be followed precisely. Anything that may be construed as insubordination may be grounds for termination.

Persuasive

Persuasive managers are similar to authoritarian managers, but put more energy into convincing their employees that orders and decisions are made in the best interest of the entire team. The slightly greater level of transparency is designed to increase trust between management and staff.

Paternalistic

Paternalistic managers act as if, in some sense, their employees are their children. That is, they explain their decisions but are highly controlling in their expectations in a way that may feel condescending.

Democratic leaders:

- *Get input from employees rather than working solely from a top-down vantage.*
- *Value and solicit employee ideas and input.*

- *Communicate both top-down and bottom-up.*

In contrast with autocratic managers, democratic leaders do not work solely from a top-down vantage, and instead get input from employees before making their final decisions. As a result, employee ideas and input are valued and even solicited. Communication is both top-down and bottom-up as a result.

Advantages of democratic management include getting more diverse perspectives and inclusive voices in the decision-making process as well as greater employee engagement; employees feel more valued because they feel heard. This can, in turn, increase productivity and motivation.

Disadvantages include the time it may take to gather input from employees as well as the potential conflicts that may arise when viewpoints differ or employees do not feel that their input has been heard. This style of management can also result in "paralysis by analysis" in some organizations.

Managers who want everyone to feel heard can sometimes become less decisive when many voices speak on a topic, process, or change. I've also seen this type of management style be taken advantage of by employees who are more prone to opinion than action.

Varieties of democratic management include:

- *Collaborative*
- *Consultative*
- *Participative*

Collaborative

In collaborative management, managers seek out a consensus. One drawback, however, is that the opinion of the majority may not always be what is actually best for the business.

Consultative

In consultative management, managers still seek out employees' opinions, but ultimately only consider those opinions as extra information in making their decisions.

Participative

Participative management can be the most involved, and may give employees more say, but has the drawback that not all employees may want to be as responsible for helping make managerial decisions.

Laissez-faire leaders:

- *Are least involved in day-to-day operations.*
- *Give their employees the greatest autonomy.*
- *Work best with highly skilled and highly motivated workers.*
- *Work best in organizations with less hierarchy, or where employees are as skilled as management.*

Laissez-faire managers are the most hands-off when it comes to overseeing their employees, and as a result, are least involved in day-to-day operations and give their employees the greatest autonomy. This works best for highly skilled employees who are also highly motivated and who do not need much in the way of supervision, as they can handle problem-solving and decision-making as needed.

This tends to work best in organizations with less hierarchy, or in situations where the staff may be as skilled (or more so) than management. As a result, this type of management allows employees to innovate as needed. While that innovation can be advantageous to your organization, laissez-faire management can also run the risk of directionless work or low productivity as the result of lacking oversight. In some organizations, it results in "too many cooks in the kitchen," which then translates into inconsistency in process, action, and decision making.

Varieties of laissez-faire management include:

- *Delegative management*
- *Bossless environments*
- *Self-managed teams.*

Delegative Management

Delegative managers do just that—they delegate. They assign tasks as needed, but generally trust that their employees do not need oversight or greater direction beyond the original assigning of tasks. This gives a great degree of autonomy and authority to employees, which can be great for highly skilled teams but can be catastrophic when team members lack the requisite skills for the tasks to which they are assigned.

Bossless Environments And Self-Managed Teams

Bossless environments and self-managed teams may limit the management by taking positions out of the organizational hierarchy, so that employees may report to a director, for instance, rather than any sort of manager. These environments simply do not work

157

for most organizations because of the level of skill and motivation required for such autonomous employees to be effective, but can work in instances where the employees are highly educated, self-directed, and either more skilled or more knowledgeable than management.

Management By Walking Around

Similarly to laissez-faire management, some managers may practice what is sometimes referred to as "management by walking around." Managers who practice this leadership style believe that interpersonal communication is key to employee engagement. The increased visibility of this management style can help keep employees stay engaged, provided that managers don't appear to be working less or holding unreasonable expectations; such appearances can result in employee dissatisfaction. Similarly, frequent managerial appearances can be distracting for employees.

In conclusion, each management style has its place. Leaning on a single, dominant style will create a lopsided organization in terms of decision making, accountability, and organizational culture. As people and situations vary, so should your management style. Identify what style you lean towards, become self-aware of when and how you use it, and consciously study and apply alternate management styles as situations dictate. Over time you will learn to seamlessly move from one style to another and will find it conducive to more rapidly making the changes, and developing the employees, that the organization needs.

Chapter 15: Evaluating Your Management Style

For most of us, our management style varies depending on the context, whether that's specific employees, specific tasks, or even a specific shop.

Beyond that, the aforementioned management styles are just broad schools of thought. Very few managers anymore fit neatly into just one box.

The point remains, however, that to be an effective manager you need to know your preferred management style so that you can modify and adapt as needed.

And there's no shame in not naturally knowing what your management style is or how to clarify how you manage. Often, when surveyed, more than half of all managers cannot identify their management style.

161

Similarly, nearly two-thirds of all managers have become managers without any sort of management training, meaning many of us manage entirely by feel.

That isn't to say that managing by feel is a bad thing. After all, if you've worked your way up from floor sweeper to a management position, you're often much more familiar with the work needed at each step of the ladder to where you are now, and that familiarity is one of your best tools as a boss. You can rely on your own personal experiences as you manage others.

But the best management is also informed by knowledge outside of just individual experience, and that's where learning your management style and how to adapt it to the needs of your workplace really comes in handy.

After all, a huge part of learning how to make others better—which, it might be said, is one of the biggest pieces of being a good manager in any workspace— is understanding both your own natural style of management and how to adapt what comes most naturally to you to the needs of your individual employees.

Being a good manager often means learning, or knowing, how to make others better.

Toward that end, there are countless tests online that can give you an idea of how you naturally best relate to your employees, each of which uses different terms and descriptions. Try a couple of them to get a sense for different ways of looking objectively at your own management style, as you may identify more with one result than another.

(If you're looking for suggestions, a couple of my favorites are the tests available from MindTools.com, Idealist Careers, and the Harvard Business Review.) For instance, one management test may identify you as a Diplomat, while another may call you a Planner. The two test results may say very similar things about your management style but do so in different ways.

As a result, using a couple of different tests can give you a more comprehensive and better sense of your management style by looking at it from a few different angles.

Don't overthink this step, though. Find a few sites you trust and use them to figure out which management traits are your defining characteristics. Perhaps you lean toward a collaborative model, or conversely, perhaps you prefer individualized management. Are you overbearing or relaxed? These are the sorts of things you'll need to consider and identify for yourself.

Advantages of knowing your natural management style:

- *Knowing your management style helps you appeal to others.*
- *Knowing your management style can help you adapt to employees' needs.*
- *Recognizing your natural management style can better help you address your weaknesses.*
- *Aware managers are more able to engage their employees.*
- *Aware managers don't need to incorporate fads.*
- *Aware managers can manage more effectively.*

Once you have a sense of your style—as well as any auxiliary management styles you may naturally utilize, as we are rarely the exact same manager day-in and day-out, and how we manage various groups of individuals may also vary widely—you can use this information in quite a few ways to become a more effective manager. Remember, knowledge is power, but the application of that knowledge is even more powerful.

Remember, knowledge is power, but the application of that knowledge is even more powerful.

Knowing Your Management Style Helps You Appeal To Others

This works both ways. First, knowing your management style can help you when interviewing for positions up the ladder (if you aren't already running the show, that is). Having a firm grasp of how you relate to current subordinates or future employees is a huge part of showing you know what you are doing.

Second, it can help you when you are hiring. Not only will prospective employees appreciate your transparency if you can be clear with them in the interview process about your management style, but that transparency can help you ask pointed questions in the interview to find individuals who will best fit with both your needs and your management style.

Understanding your primary management style can help you ask interview questions that result in finding individuals who best fit your organizational needs and management style.

As a result, being able to clearly explain how you manage makes you both a more appealing hire and a more appealing boss.

Knowing Your Management Style Can Help You Adapt To Employees' Needs.

Knowing your management style can help you understand a little more clearly, too, why you might be struggling to reach an employee. Similarly, if you've just taken a new position or are otherwise transitioning into an environment where a team is already in place with a system that works for them, recognizing your natural management style can help you intuitively see the places where you may need to adjust to better accommodate systems and individuals that work better under a different management style.

Some teams or individuals may need more direct oversight, whereas others may work best when left to work autonomously and with minimal management. Recognizing how your natural management style can either help or hinder these individuals can help you adapt your approach to help get the most of them, just as tweaking your management style can sometimes help reengage an underperforming team or employee.

This is one of the fastest ways to improve as a manager, too, and it's an area in which we should always be looking for ways to grow.

An integral part of being a successful manager of people and teams is recognizing how to blend a variety of managerial styles, depending on the context in which you are managing.

An integral part of being a successful manager of people and teams is recognizing how to blend a variety of managerial styles depending on the context in which you are managing, whether that is project-dependent, based on individual employee needs, or even time of year or other factors outside of your control.

Recognizing your natural management style can better help you address your weaknesses.

By now you should well know that you are not perfect. Nor will you ever be perfect. Just as every leader before you and every leader after you, you have blind spots.

For instance, perhaps the management style surveys you participated in identified you as an "Energizer" type of manager. That can be great for building enthusiasm and getting people going, but it might not be as great for those times when you need to slow down and gather input from others. Your go-go-go manner of management, if you are this type of manager, may make it difficult to recognize when members of your team need a little more support or have ideas that may conflict with your own. An excited and energetic manager can also run into issues where they are perceived as a steamroller, for instance, if they are not careful about addressing their natural weak spots.

If you are aware of your weak areas and consciously focus on them, you can work to actively
improve as a manager.

If you are aware of your weak areas, though, and consciously focus on them, you can work to actively

167

improve as a manager, which is all our employees can really ask of us—that we are there for them and that just as we ask them to grow and challenge themselves, we do the same for ourselves.

Aware managers are more able to engage their employees.

When it comes to business buzzwords, few have gotten more traction in recent years than engagement—and with good reason.

Engaged employees are happier, more effective, and contribute to a positive organizational culture.

Engaged employees are happier, more effective, and contribute to a positive organizational culture. These are great things, and they all factor into a better bottom line. Conversely, disengaged employees are not only more likely to leave, but can cost their company dearly, as we'll see in future chapters.

Your management style has a direct impact on how engaged your employees are with their work.

Your management style has a direct impact on how engaged your employees are with their work. If they feel comfortable coming to you with questions, concerns, suggestions, or ideas, they'll be more likely to feel engaged and more likely to stick around. If they are worried about being overruled, mocked, dismissed, or disregarded, they'll slowly but surely shut down.

Not only is that a loss for them and for the company, but it will reflect poorly on you and prevent you from achieving your own goals as a manager.

As a result, being aware of your management style can help you better see those places where your management is helping employees engage with their work, as well as the places where you may be negatively contributing to workplace culture and engagement.

Recognizing those places in the first step to improving on them. Developing a level of self-awareness that allows you to adapt your management style to situations and people is something the really good managers do well. This self-awareness alone can change your organization for the better.

Aware managers don't need to incorporate fads.

Knowing how you naturally manage best means you don't need to feel compelled to change how you lead based on each new podcast you hear or magazine article you read. Knowing how you manage means recognizing what has worked for you in the past, and what has not, which means you're less likely to constantly change how you manage your employees.

Don't confuse this, however, with an unwillingness to change and adapt as needed.

You can both maintain what has worked for you in the past and what fits with your natural management style and develop and incorporate new strategies that make you a better and more effective manager.

Your management style should both stand the test of time and adapt naturally. Toeing that line is hard, and it's one of the places where those of us with more experience sometimes run into trouble. We know what has worked for us in the past and can be resistant to adaptation and change.

So recognize that you can and should stick with what has worked for you and fits with your natural management style—and you can adapt and utilize new strategies as needed to fit the needs of your organization and your employees.

Recognizing this need for balance can make you a more efficient and effective manager, allowing you to better support your team members so they too can function at their best, pushing themselves forward, learning and growing.

Aware managers can manage more effectively.

Discovering your own personal management style additionally allows you to move forward with confidence, flexibility, and self-awareness, all of which can, in turn, help you become a more effective manager.

We've talked in significantly more depth in the previous chapters about the skills required to be a successful manager, and those that will help limit turnover, promote growth, and manage teams successfully, but I wanted to point out that thinking about your own personal management style should be at the forefront of your mind as you continue your journey towards managerial excellence.

Recognize that what works for someone else may not be what works for us.

Finally, we each have to recognize that what works for someone else may not be what works for us, and as such, I think the knowledge you've just gained about your natural management style can be incredibly helpful to you. The trick is not to change who you are, but to grow and adapt with a purpose.

Chapter 16: Accountability Tools

Knowing your management style, setting expectations and having a core organizational philosophy is one thing, and will take some work to get dialed in. As you build your managerial skills, however, holding people accountable is a really important step in leveling up. Fortunately for you, there are certain tools that can be used to help hold people accountable and which can help you level up faster.

Let's take some time to familiarize yourself with different tools and strategies you can use, allowing you to, in time, find what works best with your natural managerial style.

We talked a bit about management styles in Chapter 14, but let's quickly recap because your managerial style will go a long way in helping determine which accountability tools work best for you.

In Chapter 14, we looked at some of the major management styles, including autocratic, democratic, and laissez-faire. We also noted that most likely you won't use the same management style in every situation and that you will need to adapt and modify your approach with experience. But knowing what comes most naturally to you can help you modify and adapt more successfully, allowing you to build on your strengths and more consciously develop your weaknesses. So if you haven't taken the time yet, please do put in the time to learn more about your natural management style and what you can do to supplement in those areas where your natural management tendencies can use some additional support.

Beyond that, though, I also want you to think about how your management style can and should lend itself well to accountability in your employees.

Accountability-driven management:

- *Management should drive accountability.*
- *If you step in to fix things for your employees, you are not helping them build accountability or skills. You are enabling.*
- *Enabling is not accountability-driven management.*

- *Telling someone they're doing something wrong and then doing it for them is not helping them learn how to do it right.*
- *Instead, learn to coach your teams. Help them take ownership of their mistakes.*
- *Discuss mistakes and necessary improvements in a way that helps employees take ownership of their actions.*

If it isn't already clear, the style in which you manage can, in and of itself, create accountability. If you are one of those managers who steps in and fixes things every time you see something being done in a way you don't want it to be done—first, I fully understand, having been there myself, but second, you're not helping your employees grow and learn. And you're not putting yourself in a position to be able to work *on* the business, rather you are ensuring you will continue to work *in* the business.

Good managers don't enable. Instead, they coach, teach, and hold employees accountable for their mistakes.

When you step in and do work for your employees, you are not holding them accountable. Instead, you are enabling them. Good managers don't enable. Instead, they coach, teach, and hold employees accountable for their mistakes. If we as managers simply make the corrections for them, the lesson they take is that we'll fix their mistakes. That's not the lesson we want our employees taking from corrective interactions, because it doesn't actually hold them accountable for their actions.

Instead, we're far better off if we give direction, guidelines, and expectations, and know that as employees make mistakes we will need to hold them accountable for those mistakes, coach their abilities so they know exactly where they made their mistakes and can own those mistakes, and help them avoid the mistakes in the future by giving them the support they need to take ownership of the process.

Employees that expect you to fix their mistakes are a problem.

Employees that need coaching aren't a problem (and we'll, in fact, spend more time on coaching in the next chapter). Employees that expect you to fix their mistakes, however, are a problem. So use your management skills and the organizational culture you've helped build to help hold employees accountable as part of your organizational culture. Build accountability into your core organizational philosophy. Help make learning and growth core tenants for all employees and they can better help hold themselves accountable.

Good managers teach their employees the process they want and how to think their way through the process and any associated challenges.

If we coach employees, they can learn and grow. If we do their work for them, fixing their mistakes, we're teaching them they don't have to own their work, and that's the wrong lesson. Instead, we want to teach them how to execute the processes we want, how to think their way through challenges, and how to make good decisions. Over time they'll become better, more valuable employees than we ever could have imagined at the onset.

When we hire well, we hire capable employees who can grow and learn. Using accountability and coaching helps employees take ownership of their work.

The Value Of Metrics And Processes

We must have something to hold our employees accountable to, of course, besides just our word. We've already discussed how "because I said so" is not a valid management tool, and that's just as true when it comes to accountability.

If employees don't understand the expectation because it hasn't been clearly communicated, that is on us. We can avoid that problem, however, by clearly communicating our expectations with metrics and documentation.

Metrics, documented processes, or clearly delineated processes are each objective enough

177

*that it is hard for employees to deny knowing
what you meant.*

Accountability and communicating expectations is also a place where specificity comes in handy, especially as it can help you and your employees understand precisely where disconnects or misunderstandings may be arising when there are issues.

Keep in mind, too, that this is different than expecting that everything is done exactly the way you would do it. If the results are there, but the steps the employee took were different than the ones you would have taken, that doesn't have to be a cause of problems. There are plenty of instances in which technicians and service advisors get the results I need from them but may have gotten there in a slightly different way than I would have—and that's okay. Remember, our brains don't all work the same way.

The important part, for me, is that those employees have taken ownership of the process and hold themselves accountable—because they know what the expectation is and they have taken charge of that expectation. Knowing what they will be measured against helps them choose an appropriate path for change and growth. Whenever you can, provide a metric for which to measure progress against, ensure they understand the factors involved in the metric, and consistently remind the employee that you are watching that metric.

Consistency In Communication

No matter how many times I say this—and I'll return to it in Chapter 21 when I focus specifically on the importance of consistency—I cannot say it enough: You must be consistent in your communication. This means both what you say and what you do. If you have an expectation of timeliness, for instance, but only sometimes enforce it, you are not helping hold your team accountable. Similarly, if you have an expectation of timeliness, but you yourself are not on-time, you also have a problem—because you do not have consistency in messaging when you are telling your people they have to be in the shop at a certain time but you aren't there yourself. As a manager I always made it a point to be the first one in the building, and the last one to leave. Did I always want to be? No! I felt that the message it sent to the employees I was asking excellence from was very important, however.

(A note here: There will be times when you may need to be in a meeting elsewhere or have other valid reasons for not being in the shop when you expect your employees to be there. Being transparent with your team and being consistent in your communication with them can go a long way in helping ensure this doesn't become a point of contention later.)

Another part of consistent communication is not waiting to address problem issues.

Another part of consistent communication is not waiting to address problem issues. This doesn't always mean calling someone out on the spot—blasting an employee in front of their peers can be demeaning, after all, even if it isn't meant that way, and as a result, isn't always the most effective way of holding them accountable, for instance—but it does not mean putting off addressing issues.

If, for instance, you have an employee that shows up late, you can wait until there is a quiet moment later when you can pull them aside individually to discuss the problem behavior in a way that demonstrates that you value and respect them as an employee and a person, but also need them to live up to the expectations everyone has agreed to as part of the job and as an organizational standard. This allows you to be firm and fair with your employees without degrading them as people.

Good managers help employees connect their actions with the results or consequences of those actions.

Similarly, be sure to help employees connect their actions with the results or consequences of those actions. If they are late, for instance, who had to pick up their slack, or how did that contribute to a work order not being fulfilled on time? If they made a mistake in a process, who was responsible for catching that mistake and what did that time and labor cost the shop, for instance? If information was

180

missing on a form, how did that affect the service advisors' (or techs') ability to do their job well given that missing information?

Helping employees connect the dots and see what results from their actions can help them take ownership, and whatever consequences you need to include as a manager should fit the problem behavior and the relationship you have with that employee, including how many strikes they might already have and so forth. Ideally, this is written into your HR processes.

If it isn't part of your organizational structure, you can still be consistent in your communication, of course. In no circumstances should employees get differential treatment as that is often construed as favoritism. Being consistent in your communication means a third strike should be treated the same for each employee that is late for the third time, for instance, but being late three times is not the same as making mistakes that might make a vehicle unsafe to drive. Not every problem is created equal. Just make sure that your messaging and consequences are consistent to the situation, and you'll be well on your way—and as you continue to grow, do take the step of sitting down and codifying all of this within your HR practices.

Not to belabor the point, but here's the thing: I know this might sound like a strange analogy, but sometimes managing employees is like training a puppy—you can't wait very long before communicating what the problem is and how you expect it fixed. Similarly, just as the tone you use with a puppy can tell them everything they need to know, the tone with which you address problem behaviors communicates a great deal to your employees.

Employees can have rather short memories, and if the action is not connected with the result and consequences, learning may not take place.

When you find or see something wrong, pick the next appropriate time to have a discussion about what needs to be different. Use your core organizational philosophy to frame what was wrong and why the behavior needs to change, and point out any documentation that might represent their previous understanding of what the expected behavior was in that situation.

Don't let behavior you don't want to go too long unaddressed, nor should you let frustration build up before addressing it. No good will come of putting the discussion off—even if that might be easier in the short-term—nor are you as likely to be specific with your feedback if you wait too long to have the discussion.

The best communication is consistent. The same message over and over again will eventually be heard.

The best communication is consistent. The same message over and over again will eventually be heard.

Employee Reviews

An employee review process helps to ensure consistent communication and goal setting. These yearly or even quarterly reviews can help create a huge amount of accountability. If you do not already have a yearly employee review process, you need to get one implemented as soon as possible.

Goals, performance reviews, and regular one-on-one check-in meetings (whether formal or informal) create a great deal more accountability than in shops where managers simply give directives and then shut themselves in their office. Just knowing someone is looking, discussing, checking, and watching their work can create accountability for many employees.

Your review process should include:

- Employee self-evaluation.
- Manager evaluation.
- Previous goals and milestones.
- Future goals and milestones.
- Regular check-ins to monitor progress.

If you need help implementing an employee review process, reach out to me at www.rsrcoach.com and I'll get you started.

When things like reviews are regularly used, it makes the manager's job much easier and less frustrating. Consistency is the key, though! (One way to help develop that consistency is to make performance reviews and regular one-on-one check-in meetings part of your HR processes.)

Documentation

Documentation:

- *Helps to flesh your processes out.*
- *Helps streamline and organize procedures and policies.*
- *Can become a training tool.*
- *Can certainly be used as an accountability tool.*

Consistency means documentation.

Part of consistency should be documentation. No matter how good your brain, you cannot remember every time you have given employees direction, nor how that direction was given, if there is no documentation.

Similarly, documentation can help team members adhere to process and can help enforce consistency in setting and addressing expectations, which can greatly aid accountability.

Documenting significant processes, procedures, and methods can be a great tool. The documentation becomes a way of making sure you have the process that you really want. Once you write something down, it's easier to see what will work and what you need to continue working on. When you have the documentation, you also now have a tool for training new hires, a tool to modify the process or procedures as needed in the future, and a tool for accountability. Having an employee sign off on the procedure after training makes it an even stronger accountability tool.

Use Signatures

Related to that, signatures can be a strong psychological tool for creating buy-in. Use documentation for training, give the employee the process or procedure in writing, have them practice the process or procedure, and then have them sign off that they understand the process or procedure and possess the skills required to do it correctly. This alone creates accountability, but also becomes an HR tool if something goes wrong and you need to prove a lack of accountability or otherwise protect yourself or your shop from the actions of an employee.

Signatures:

- ***Are a way to help get employees to fully commit to a process or procedure.***

- *Can be a powerful accountability tool.*
- *Can also protect you if you need to later prove documentation.*

Meetings

Everyone hates meetings. It's a simple, universal truth. Most of us hate them because we consider them a waste of time; they rarely seem to accomplish much, and they pull us away from the parts of our job we'd rather spend our time and energy on.

Yet consistent, well-conducted meetings can be a great accountability tool. Knowing that I'll have to explain how things are going, what our numbers are (and what we're doing about making those numbers better), as well as our direction for the future, can create motivation to look good. Seeing other employees held accountable for their words, actions, and promises also keeps me motivated to stay accountable. It's a gentle stress and pressure that keeps the system moving.

Never underestimate the power of consistent, well-organized meetings.

Don't let meetings get too long; if at all possible, keep them under 20 minutes and stick to a predetermined agenda. Let the key attendees know ahead of time what you want to discuss and what they should come prepared to show or discuss themselves. Regularly scheduled meetings—monthly, for instance, seems to work well, though some shops do weekly or bi-weekly—should be held with all department heads, even if that department head is the entire department! Never underestimate the power of consistent, well-organized meetings for helping keep everyone on the same page and for helping keep people accountable to common goals and more.

Connect The Dots

Similarly, make sure your employees are connecting the dots between pieces of information and processes. When team members know why the process is designed the way it is, and why the policy is the way it is, and how those policies and processes are connected to the core organizational philosophy, they can really buy in and invest and engage—all things that can help hold everyone in the organization accountable toward that core organizational philosophy.

Setting expectations and holding employees accountable is important. Without coaching skills (which we'll address in greater depth in the next chapter), however, that isn't enough. Expectations and accountability help employees know what to do consistently, but don't help when they don't have the skills. So use coaching to help connect the dots.

Everything functions together in a system. Organizations are complex systems that require constant attention; employees need skill development; managers need management training; technicians need technical training and everyone needs motivating.

Everything functions together in a system. Your organization is a complex system that requires constant attention. Employees need skill development. Managers need management training. Technicians need technical training. And everyone needs motivating. It all works together. Setting expectations, holding employees accountable, having a core organizational philosophy, and documenting important processes are all good—but without coaching skills, it is rarely enough. So make sure you and your employees are developing the coaching skills they need.

Which brings us to our next chapter...

Chapter 17: Coaching

Coaching is necessary for and in any organization. Coaching is not telling, or showing, but rather guiding. Many shop owners and managers tell me things like, "but I shouldn't have to."

Fine. Maybe you shouldn't have to coach your employees in a perfect world. But that isn't the world we live in, and no matter how many applicants you get for each open position, no matter how well you hire, you will have employees that need coaching. That's simply reality, so rather than fight it, why not put your energy toward doing a good job of coaching your team up? Think about it. Even professional athletes still need coaches.

No matter how selective you are in hiring, you won't hire people that are just like you.

No two people are alike, and no matter how selective you are in hiring, you won't hire people that are just like you or will know exactly what you like. That's just something you're going to have to get over.

Get Over Yourself

I want you to start by thinking of those attributes in other people—maybe even some of your employees—you hate.

Write it down, or hold it in your head for a moment. Why do you hate it? Does hating that thing work to develop people or their skills?

If you're being honest with yourself, you know it doesn't, so let it go.

Same with managing. Are there parts of managing you hate? If you're like me, there probably are, but that doesn't mean you can just avoid them.

Here's the truth plenty of managers don't want to accept: To be a great manager, you have to get over yourself. There are going to be things you don't want to do, but that doesn't mean you don't have to still do them. That's just part of running a business and managing a team or teams of people.

To be a great manager, you have to get over yourself.

So think of the things that drive you nuts, and then just let them go.

A trick that helps some managers? Remember that some of those tasks that you really don't like are part of your core organizational philosophy. Sometimes that reminder helps make them less unpleasant because you're better able to put them in the larger context for yourself.

Coaching 101

- **Good coaching requires careful word choices.**
- **Good coaching is objective, not emotional.**
- **Good coaching deals with specific facts; the more specific those facts, the better.**
- **Good coaching is good teaching and includes repetition to help students learn.**

Coaching Skills

Coaching is more about using the right words at the right time than anything else. You can show someone how to do something all you want, but until they do it themselves, find out what it feels like, get to ask questions, and then mess it up, they will never learn it. When you've done something your entire career, and it is simple and easy to you, it feels like you're wasting your time when someone "just doesn't get it." This is where the skill of coaching comes in.

You need to recognize that there are many learning styles that may come into play when coaching.

For instance, it can be hard to maintain objectivity. After all, if you're running your own shop you're probably pretty passionate about the work and the organization you've built; it can be easy to get frustrated. But emotions don't have a place while coaching employees—whether that emotion is frustration, anger, exasperation, or whatever you might be feeling. Calm, collected, patient, empathetic, and understanding will get you further when coaching.

It can take a person many more times than twice to actually understand what needs to happen or to learn a new skill.

For most people, it can readily take at least three times to learn a new skill or up to 40 days to adopt a new habit.

Positivity

When it comes to coaching, positivity can go a long way toward setting an employee at ease and allowing them to be coachable. A recent article from the Harvard Business Review, for instance, suggested that the single best thing you can do for employees is to show them encouragement and give recognition.

A recent article from the Harvard Business Review, for instance, suggested that the single best thing you can do for employees is to show them encouragement and give recognition.

Just like how when you're selling service from a courtesy inspection you always lead with the good stuff, you should do the same when coaching employees. One way to work is with a praise sandwich: Lead with praise (or a positive piece of encouragement), follow with the bit of criticism (provided it is gentle, specific, and objective), and then close with praise or encouragement.

To be an effective coach, you need employees to feel strong and capable of learning, changing, and progressing. Anything you do or say to them that makes them think they are less than worthless will not get you what you need.

Positivity:

- *A positive attitude can go a long way in setting a good tone for effective coaching.*
- *Positive expectations for success, such as "I know you can…," or "I like the way you…" can be affirming.*

- *When handing out criticism or critiquing performance, be gentle yet firm, leading and closing with positive encouragements.*
- *Always lead with the positive.*

Exercising Restraint

As a technician, I was often boisterous, loud, aggressive, and angry most of the time. I learned early in my career that this was a good way to ensure I kept other people from slowing down my production or otherwise getting in my way. If I was constantly grumpy, nobody would ask me for help! Of course, this isn't exactly a skill set conducive to management excellence!

Fortunately, it didn't take me too long to learn that wasn't the way I wanted to act if I wanted to be a good manager and coach. Not all managers pick up that lesson quite as quickly. If this is you—if you've risen the ranks in part because of your ability to keep other people out of your way, this is something you'll need to work at to become a better manager and especially to become a better coach.

I had to learn a different way of being and acting if I wanted to effectively manage and coach.

Developing other people, all the way from students working on internships to grizzled veterans learning management skills, requires we exercise restraint sometimes (along with a healthy dose of patience). Our natural reactions aren't always helpful, so learning how to catch that natural reaction and hold it back can help us become better managers and coaches.

For instance, when you see something done poorly or incorrectly, the knee jerk reaction "what are you doing?" may not be the best idea. Learn restraint and calmness. Learn to keep things objective and less emotional. It won't always be easy, and this doesn't mean ignoring what is going on until it builds up and you explode. It simply means practicing control over your emotions, and learning to use words and phrases, so that you can deal with any situation that may arise calmly and rationally, so you can better manage and coach your employees.

Exercising restraint:

- *Reacting is not always best.*
- *Restraint gives you time to develop a more rational and objective perspective.*
- *Keeping things more objective and rational allows you to better coach and manage.*

Coaching By Example

As a manager, acting as a coach, you'll want to lead by example. It's really hard to get someone to do

195

something they've never done before (especially if don't have their experiences, either) or to convince them you know best.

One of the strongest and most effective ways you can coach is often to coach by example.

As a result, one of the strongest and most effective ways you can coach is often to coach by example.

If you can be willing to try out a new skill or process for yourself, to jump into the situation fully, it allows you to better understand what the employee is seeing and feeling. It also shows them that you're willing to do precisely what it is you're asking them to do. Leading by example in this way is often one of the most effective coaching strategies you can put in your arsenal.

A word of caution, however: *Coaching by example is not the same as doing something for someone else.* You are just sending the message that you are in it with them, not for them. All too often managers who are still getting their feet underneath them make this mistake, misunderstanding leading by example to mean that they should do things for their employees. "I'm just showing them how to do it," they might rationalize—but that's a slippery slope.

Coaching by example is not the same as doing something for someone else.

When coaching by example, show your employees how to do the task or process the way it should be done—and then have them practice. Watch them the first few times so you can give pointers, sure, but don't step back in. They need to learn by doing. Let them do, provide feedback, and let them do some more. Don't forget the importance of metrics!

If you follow these guidelines, you can be a great coach. Be willing to change, be good to your word, meet deadlines, and do what you say you're going to do—these are all ways of leading and coaching by example, too.

Coaching by example:

- **Lead with your example, and be willing to demonstrate new skills as you coach them.**
- **Try not to ask your employees to do something you haven't yourself done.**
- **Your willingness to try, do, and see for yourself sends a message to your employees.**
- **Don't confuse coaching by example with doing someone else's work for them.**

Incorporating inclusivity in your coaching and managing.

We've hinted at the magic of including others in decision-making as part of your managerial processes in other chapters, but I want to reiterate how inclusivity can empower your coaching and managing.

The better the job you do of including others, the more engaged and invested those same people are likely to be in the decisions you make.

The truth is, the better the job you do of including others, the more engaged and invested those same people are likely to be in the decisions you together make. When you are coaching someone, including them in the coaching process can only make it more effective. This isn't the same as asking an employee to design their own coaching, of course, but including them—especially in process development, in the documentation of process, tracking metrics, providing feedback, etc—in the steps of their coaching journey helps put them in the driver's seat and encourages them to develop.

Inclusive coaching can be much more collaborative, allowing you to better find coaching strategies that might work for the entire team.

Many of the best solutions arise when everyone contributes to solve a problem or find a way forward.

Many of the best solutions arise when everyone contributes to solve a problem or find a way forward; as often as not, the whole truly is greater than the sum of its parts. Inclusive and collaborative coaching can also help shape organizational culture, help you reconnect your work to the core organizational philosophy, and help create a natural mentoring system between peers as some individuals pick up certain skills or processes faster than others.

Inclusive coaching:

- **People buy-in and are more engaged when they are included.**
- **Many times the best solutions arise as a result of asking employees for their suggestions on problem resolution.**
- **Empowers employees to take initiative.**
- **Affirms your core organizational philosophy and can help create natural mentoring possibilities.**

Motivational Coaching

And then, of course, there's motivational coaching. Depending on your natural managerial style, this may be very easy and come very naturally for you. Or it may prove incredibly difficult.

Some managers are naturally charismatic and can easily motivate their employees. If that's you, great. For many of us, though, this is something we have to work on.

A few pointers: Motivation works best when it is genuine. And that doesn't mean sarcasm or flippancy, either; as before, the best way to motivate people is with energetic and authentic positivity.

Use positive affirmations, recognition and celebration of success, and reward breakthroughs to help build people up when they have done well.

Use positive affirmations, recognition and celebration of success, along with rewarding breakthroughs to help build people up when they have done well. Be sure to do so consistently—this is another place where favoritism can all too readily rear its ugly head—and be sure to do so kindly, without diminishing other employees who perhaps have not had the same success.

If you can do those things you're well on your way to learning how to motivate your employees. The rest will vary depending on your natural managerial style; you do, after all, have to manage in a way that is authentic and genuine to you in order to be effective.

Motivate by:

- *Using positive affirmations such as "you've done exactly what we wanted to see."*
- *Recognizing and celebrating success.*

- *Rewarding breakthroughs and milestone achievements.*
- *Affirming employees who embody the organizational philosophy.*

What Works For You?

The best coaching blends these strategies in a way that is authentic and genuine to you, your core organizational philosophy, and the needs of your employees.

Just remember:
- *Be positive.*
- *Exercise restraint.*
- *Set an example.*
- *Be inclusive.*
- *Motivate.*

If you can do each of those things, you're well on your way to becoming a great coach.

Chapter 18: Communication

The importance of communication when it comes to managing cannot be overemphasized. Communication between employees or within the organization as a whole must be clear and consistent. Often, I see owners who are more comfortable with organizational communication—such as communicating processes or problems to the entire group—than they are with individual communication. Unfortunately for those managers, the skill of individual communication is often more important to your organization than the ability to communicate with everyone at once. Think of it like this: When you want to get really good at something, it's important to get the details right than to look at the big picture right away.

The skill of individual communication is often more important to your organization than the ability to communicate with everyone at once.

And it's the same with communicating with your team. Focus on getting really good at communicating with individuals, and the organizational culture will come with it, as will the buy-in and engagement. You need to get that stuff down as a manager, and that's one of the reasons why individual communication is so important.

Because organizational communication is often easier for new managers, though, let's start there.

Organizational Communication

Many times the entire organization gets communications from you as their manager when there is a problem. Whether this is in the form of a shop meeting, email, or text, the sad truth is this: when employees only hear bad news from the boss, they learn to hate communications from the boss. It is also hard to create a positive culture when organizational communication is always negative.

My experience has taught me that the best form of organizational communication takes the form of shop meetings.

And often enough, that negative communication can be misconstrued as well. My experience has taught me that the best form of organizational communication takes the form of shop meetings. Not only do emails and texts tend to take on a life of their own through interpretation by each individual, making them less than ideal for organizational communication, but shop meetings allow everyone to hear the same message, ask questions, and see accountability in action.

That doesn't mean shop meetings are the only option, of course—emails, process manuals, individual meetings, voicemails, and texts all have their own benefits in certain contexts—but shop meetings do have the widest application and often provide the most transparency.

Regardless of the mode of communication, though, keep in mind that you don't want to overwhelm your employees so much as ensure they get the information they need. As a result, make sure your meetings are easy to digest.

Meeting guidelines:

- *Keep them short.*
- *Keep them consistent (weekly or monthly, for instance).*
- *Keep them to the scheduled agenda.*

Shop meetings cannot and will not cover all necessary communication, however. For many types of communication, an email may be the best option. Not only does it allow for documentation via the written record (which can helpful for accountability purposes), but it also allows individuals to check their email as it best fits in their schedule, meaning it doesn't have to disrupt workflow—provided employees check their email regularly.

Email is great for things like setting holiday schedules, booking time-off requests, scheduling trainings, and more. It allows for that written record that helps ensure information doesn't get lost, and it keeps from putting people on the spot, which can happen in meetings or individual one-on-one conversations. Emails do not take the place of one-on-one conversations when it comes to solving challenges or performance issues, however.

Use email to send agendas before meetings, too, and help set the tone that employees are expected to check their email regularly. Toward that end, I advise never scheduling a meeting with less than 24 hours notice, but employees should know that they are expected to check email at least once each day—and that scheduling a few minutes a few times a day is not a bad way to stay on top of their email and to ensure they don't miss important communications. The first time someone misses a meeting because they didn't see the email reminder can be a good way to reinforce the importance of staying on top of their email.

Employees should know that they are expected to check email at least once each day.

Internal texting applications such as Slack can also be tremendously helpful in disseminating information, especially for teams that operate in multiple buildings or spread out facilities, or when a message needs to get out more quickly than is reasonable given the frequency with which employees do or do not check email.

Questions to consider as you examine your communication processes:

- *Do employees check their email? If so, how regularly? Do their email practices align with your expectations?*
- *When did you last hold a shop meeting? How often do you hold shop meetings? What are the expectations of shop meetings?*
- *How did you last document a process employees were expected to use or follow, and how was that information shared?*
- *Do you use an internal texting application, and how might it (or not) better serve your organization's communication needs?*

There are plenty of other strategies I've seen managers use for organizational communications, too. For instance, I've seen shop owners print new processes and leave pieces of paper on everyone's desk or toolbox to communicate the change. This is not effective!

Communication works both ways. Employees need a chance to acknowledge they've received and understood what you needed them to get.

Communication works both ways— employees need a chance to acknowledge they've received and understood what you needed them to get, especially if they did not have the opportunity to contribute to whatever it was in a shop meeting.

If the communication is important, be sure to deliver it both verbally and in written form—this includes email (assuming everyone is in the habit of checking it). Besides, printed fliers aren't much good when it comes to documentation you can use to help hold employees accountable. Email confirmations that a process was received and understood might, or having everyone who was present at a shop meeting sign to acknowledge that they received and understood the information may work much better from an accountability standpoint.

Using organizational communication to bolster accountability:

- *Verbal communication doesn't lend itself to documentation. Use forms that do.*
- *Communication of processes, etc, should be inclusive. Get input into process*

changes and have employees sign off on those changes before they go into effect.
- ***Have employees acknowledge receipt and understanding of new information either via written communication or signature.***

And if someone misses a meeting or doesn't confirm that they received and understand new materials or communications, hold them accountable. Don't just let it go.

Hold them accountable by having a sit-down meeting with them to discuss both why they missed the meeting and what was discussed in the meeting, or why they didn't understand the new materials so that you can coach them to the requisite understanding.

As a manager, you need everyone to understand that the expectations apply to all.

Employees will get in the habit of missing meetings or ignoring communications if they are not held accountable—and this pattern of behavior will become contagious before you know it if you don't address it immediately. The first time someone misses a meeting and gets pulled from their responsibilities to have a chat about it, the message will be sent to the entire organization that meetings are not to be missed.

Individual Communication

We addressed organizational communication first simply because it is easier. Speaking to a large group or setting expectations of a large group can be far simpler than managing individual employees via one-on-one communication. That said, individual communication is a powerful and necessary management tool and becoming adept with it is one of the keys to great management.

Each individual employee needs to feel important to the organization and connected to the organization if you want to get the most out of each employee.

One-on-one time helps with this—or can if done well—as it allows you to help individuals feel connected to the organization, both by assuring them that you do notice and care about their work and reminding them of their place in the larger organizational philosophy. This type of one-on-one communication should be part of a formal review process, and should also take place as needed via regularly scheduled check-in meetings such as with department heads, stakeholders in any new process, or new hires.

But what does that look like and how do you become adept at individual communication as a manager?

While that looks a little different for everyone, there are a few principles that can help get you started.

Guidelines for effective one-on-one communication:

- **Actively listen.**
- **Allow input and discussion.**
- **Ask questions.**
- **Be specific, especially if working to solve a problem or work through a process.**
- **Be objective; don't let things get personal and/or emotional.**
- **Keep it professional: This is about the business, not about the person. Unless there is something serious outside of work that affects performance at work, communication should focus on the organizational environment and needs.**

During this one-on-one time great managers listen actively, ask questions, are specific about behaviors or criticisms and allow input from the employee.

> **Sometimes it is more important to listen, than it is to talk.**

The adage "It is more important to be interested than interesting" can go a long way in connecting an employee to the organization, helping an employee make adjustments, and creating a positive culture of growth.

211

One challenge you will regularly face during individual communication activities is that of trying to keep things professional. Sometimes you know an employee has some negative influences outside of work that will overlap into their professional life. Remembering to keep things strictly professional and coaching the employee on separating professional from personal is very important. In many small business environments, there is too much overlap between personal and professional. I understand how this happens; however, I feel strongly that it often keeps the organization from growing.

Remember to keep things strictly professional and coach your employees on separating their professional and personal lives.

Learning to coach the professional individual without forming friendships or getting too involved in the personal side of their lives is important for an owner or manager, and we'll spend some more time with professionalism in the next chapter.

Chapter 19: Professionalism

Few things can be more difficult than taking a small shop—especially if you started by yourself or with just a few friends, for instance—and building it into a larger business without potentially hurting some friendships along the way.

We've all been there. You work with someone, get to become friends, and then something changes in either the friendship or in the working relationship that in turn screws the other one up.

When it comes to friendships and business, don't let them mix.

So here's the thing: When it comes to friendships and business, I don't let them mix. If you are a growing organization like mine is and was, there will come a day when being friends with employees will cause a

213

problem. As a result, friends need to be kept outside the organization. I know this sounds cold, yet I say it for a reason.

When the shop was small and there were only two or three of you, friendships were easy. Maybe you even hired your friends as you first start growing and needed people around you that you could trust as you scaled up. Now that the shop is bigger, though, and getting bigger still, those same friendships can get in the way. A business is a living entity and as such it grows and changes.

There is a common adage in entrepreneurship that says "what got you here, will not get you where you are going." In other words, as a business grows its needs change. Those needs are the skill sets and personalities of its employees. Not every employee you hired 10 years ago has, or will have, the required skill set for today. Things change. Friendships can hinder making the required changes. I'm often saying to clients, "Remember, this is not personal, it's business. There's a difference."

It is wise to be very careful about forming friendships with your employees.

It is my personal policy not to build friendships with employees and to keep things strictly professional. I never want a friendship to get in the way of a business decision.

And that's just one of many places where professional and personal lives can make things messy in our business, which is why I want to spend some time in this chapter to discuss professionalism and the steps you can take to help ensure your business grows in a sustainable way.

We'll jump around a little bit, but in general, everything in this chapter is designed to help ensure your shop grows in a professional way. Some sections may be more applicable to your shop than others, but all of these are areas where I've seen shops fall short, which is why I'm sharing my thoughts with you—so you don't have to fall into the same traps others have fallen into.

Assigning Titles

This probably falls under the pet peeve category for me. I see so many organizations give titles to people as a way of rewarding them for time with the shop.

Unless you are really going to give the authority, responsibility, and accountability that goes with the title, please don't give the title.

Job titles are provided for a reason. To give your longest-tenured service advisor the title of Service Manager just because they've been with you for 15 years, for instance, serves no purpose. If you really want to have a service manager (or any other

215

position) and feel that it is justified based on the volume of work and structure of your organization, then create a job description and allow anyone interested to apply and interview for the position. Never just give a position to someone based on seniority and not competence for the job position. That's not the organizational philosophy you want to represent. Just giving someone the title as a reward does not mean they wanted the actual position, can perform the job duties of the position, or are worth the money the position should pay.

Active Listening

I've talked a bit about active listening in previous chapters, but I want to address it again here because it really is just that important. Active listening is as important in managing employees as it is in dealing with customers. Active listening is a large part of professionalism. Learn to listen actively yourself and teach your employees to listen actively. Find my YouTube videos on Active Listening for more information!

Using active listening as a management tool:

- *Active listening is a necessity for effective communication and management.*
- *It takes time and effort—and sometimes requires emotion be put aside.*

- *May not come easily—especially if you are used to much of your time being caught up in putting out fires.*
- *Includes eye contact, head nodding, and other nonverbal cues.*
- *Requires reflection, i.e., saying back to the person what you heard them say to you.*

Let's start by spending a little more time with those nonverbal cues. Some of these should come naturally as you start to spend more time practicing your listening skills, but it never hurts to practice these skills as well; sometimes we need our brain to catch up to our body, and sometimes we need our body to catch up to our brain. Regardless of the other, effective active listening is something we communicate with both our brain and our body.

So, about those nonverbal cues. Start by making eye contact. This sends the message that you are listening and that what I am saying is important to you. If what you are saying to me is so important, then it's important enough to make eye contact with me.

If you are someone for whom eye contact may be uncomfortable, then practice it until you get comfortable.

Similarly, practice your head nodding. I don't mean just nod your head like crazy but do so in a way that helps the other person feel heard. This may sound silly, but there is a known psychological effect on people who see head nodding when they are talking. The person feels listened to and knows that you are hearing them. It suggests some empathy and understanding as well. Of course, keep in mind that it helps if you actually feel those things; people are genuinely smart enough to tell when you are faking it, and that can backfire on you badly.

Other nonverbal cues may include tilting your head to listen better, facial expressions in response to various pieces of information, and even the way you are standing or sitting. If this is something at which you are not naturally gifted, find someone you trust who can help you practice your nonverbal cues when practicing active listening.

It's also important that you focus on using reflection and synthesizing what you hear when you practice active listening.

Saying back to the person what you thought you heard them say to you gives them a chance to hear their words and to clarify exactly what they meant.

Reflection serves multiple purposes. Saying back to the person what you thought you heard them say to you gives them a chance to hear their words, and to clarify exactly what they meant if needed. It gives the second person a chance to clarify what they heard and put it into their own words for better understanding. It also gives you a chance to ensure that you really are understanding not just the words being said, but also the larger tone and context in which they are said. If you can try and synthesize what the other person is saying, this also shows you are trying to understand what they have to say and gives you a chance to better clarify.

Objectivity

Beyond active listening, objectivity is another hallmark skill you will need to practice as part of your professionalism. Letting your emotions get away from you isn't professional, and it can lead to poorly-made decisions as well. As a result, as hard as it can sometimes be to be objective, great managers are always objective. This is about business, numbers, and moving forward. It's never about emotions, seat-of-the-pants intuition, or personal issues.

> ***Great managers learn to set emotion aside so they can be objective.***

As mentioned previously, emotion has little place in managing. A great manager learns to set emotion aside and be objective. Setting emotion aside also allows you to better see various perspectives and be able to make adjustments if there was a way of looking at something you might have missed. This goes along with being open-minded.

If you feel yourself getting too emotional, then walk away. Choose another time to have the conversation or seek a resolution. It is far better to walk away for a while even if you think you can still be objective. Most of us wear our emotion on our face and it will get in the way of good communication if we are still feeling too strong of an emotion during our conversation.

Great managers are objective. They document, measure, and monitor everything.

They are meticulous about being objective. They can tell you exactly when, what, and how. Much thought is put into measuring outcomes and inputs. Managing this way helps take intuition out of the business and drives the organization forward based on what is real. Great managers never say "I feel like this is…." Instead, they say "Let me show you"—and base their argument on solid, objective data.

Specificity

And specificity can be a big part of that objectivity and data-driven process. When it comes to managing employees, we need specific documentation to help keep us objective and rational, just as they need it for accountability. Without the metrics, we can have a disagreement about what went on. Improvement happens when we can show exactly what goes on, what the outcome was, or what the input was. This is true of phone conversations as well. Using call logging software to record phone calls and coach employees on what words to use and what to avoid is a very powerful, objective tool. If I hear myself say something in the recording, I can't push back at you and say I didn't say that, or that you heard me wrong. This specificity can also help you lean on your core organizational philosophy when having challenging conversations. Connect everything back to this philosophy. It will help to keep things objective and keep the employee from feeling things are too personal. If you explain the reasons why things are not up to standards and use the core organizational philosophy as the standard, this will keep the conversation very objective.

Good, professional managers:

- *Don't let problem issues build up.*
- *Stay on top of potential issues—and address potential issues as soon as they become known.*
- *Are consistent in their direction and adherence to the core organizational philosophy.*
- *Understand that organizations need to be adaptable without constantly changing.*

Never let potential problems build up. I've watched shop owners let things go until they couldn't take it anymore and they just explode. This only served to teach employees that they were okay until the boss yelled. Once things calmed down, they went right back to the same practices until the next blow up. Nothing ever changed.

As a great manager, though, you won't do that. Instead, you'll address potential issues as soon as you see them, and you'll address them consistently, fairly, and professionally.

The other practice a great professional manager needs to work to avoid is the practice of having constant good ideas! Let me explain. There are those shops where the boss has at least one brilliant idea each day that then gets implemented the next day. That idea stays implemented until the next good idea—a day later. Hopefully, you can see the problem with this.

Constantly changing from one great idea to the next teaches employees to weather the storm until it passes and to never put any effort into anything.

Constantly changing from one great idea to the next teaches employees to weather the storm until it passes and to never put any effort into anything— because it will only change again next week. If you implement a change, process, or procedure, get input before making any changes, and then stick with those changes for at least several months so you can build up enough data to determine whether or not the changes worked. If you need to still make changes based on the data, make those modifications only after you have enough data and input from employees to justify the change. Don't constantly change things simply because you had another idea, because that isn't fair to your employees, nor is it objective or rational.

Establishing a level of professionalism within your organization will set a tone for how employees interact with each other, with management, and ultimately with customers. This professionalism will translate into who you hire, how the business grows, and what the community thinks of your business. Don't underestimate the effect of professionalism within your business. If managers act like a bunch of four-year-old kids by dealing with problems through tantrums, you can expect everyone to deal with daily challenges the same way. Every decision, action, and change should be made very intentionally and with the best interest of the business in mind. What benefits the business will ultimately employee people, pay them fair wages, and provide for exceptional benefit packages. Be a professional.

Chapter 20: Accommodations

As we've established previously, managing is rarely ever simple, and can sometimes be an exercise of frustration as you seem to be working in this solid gray area where nothing is for sure. Often situations will arise where the problem or solution looks obvious, but there may be far more to it than you realize.

Let me tell you a story to help illustrate my point. A few years back, an employee was set to be let go. When asked for reasons why this particular employee needed to be fired, it came to light that it was because the simplest of simple tasks could not be followed.

Since this employee was the best telephone person the organization had ever had, I was hesitant to agree with the firing. I just couldn't believe that the tasks which were not being completed were that far over this person's head that they couldn't get it right. And, as it turned out, I was right—but not in the way I thought I was going to be.

As I investigated further, by asking 'why' five times, I learned a few things. As it happened, the employee in question had some learning disabilities that could have easily been overcome with better coaching and proper accommodations, yet in this case, they were being exacerbated by a feeling of being intimidated by their manager.

A side note: This intimidation was strictly a personality thing, and nothing intentional—but that doesn't make it any less problematic.

Fortunately, there was an easy solution. We put the employee in question under a different manager and scaffolded their job description a little bit to account for the learning challenges, and voila, we had a wholly different situation: Instead of replacing an employee who was seemingly underperforming, we were able to accommodate that employee's learning disability in a way that instead gave us an employee that customers loved, and someone who could more than adequately get the job done—all without the pain of turnover.

All too often, managers are unwilling to look at the underlying issues and try to solve them.

All too often, though, managers are unwilling to look at the underlying issues and try to solve them, whether that's through coaching, accommodations as appropriate, or finding a better fit for the employee elsewhere in the shop. Managing takes time, effort, and thought. Managing is not what most people think of when they envision a manager sitting in an office, or walking around telling people what to do. There are nuances and unseen challenges to be a manager, including challenges most people will never see.

For instance, sometimes we make a hire that just isn't going to work out for a given position. What if that person has different skill sets than you thought when you first interviewed and hired them? After getting to know them and their skill set better, can you find a place for them where their skill set will be used appropriately? If this person shows up for work on time, fits in terms of personality, is good with customers, goes above and beyond, but just can't produce quality work, how can you leverage what they are good at? Often times your job as a manager is to put people in the best position to succeed. You may have hired them for a specific position, but that doesn't mean they aren't more suited for a different one.

Never let a good employee go just because they cannot do the job they were first hired for. Good employees—by which I mean employees who are timely, helpful, great with customers, and who don't ever miss work, for instance—are hard to come by, so don't waste them by getting stuck in the train of thought that they can only fit in the position for which you originally hired them.

A great manager understands and gets to know their employees—and that includes getting to know how their skill sets might translate in other positions. They find those other skill sets, or interests, that maybe were not known at the time of initial hire, and then they capitalize on that knowledge.

A great manager understands and gets to know their employees—and that includes getting to know how their skill sets might translate in other positions.

For instance, we had a technician a few years back that was terrible at diagnostics. He actually didn't make a very good technician at all, as his work quality was lacking as well. His personality was great, he had the technical knowledge, and he liked the organization—all the great things you look for in an employee. Unfortunately, though, those attributes just didn't translate into being a good production technician who could produce quality work.

Instead of letting him go after his last comeback, though, we were able to move him into a parts role that to this day suits him very well. And these are the sorts of stories you, as a great manager, can accumulate, too.

The last topic I want to address in this chapter is how to handle that employee that is constantly taking advantage of the system. The employee who is always calling out sick, forgetting that they had an appointment today, or requesting a day off here, an hour there, or some sort of special accommodation. Business is business, but it also crosses that gray line where people and their personal lives intersect with it.

As a business you cannot be so rigid as to let people learn to hate working for you. You also cannot be so lenient that employees hold the business back because of what goes on in their personal lives. This is a fine line as a manager. The generations we hire today are not as given to handing over their lives to work as generations in the past were. They value their personal lives, and personal time. This can be a challenge for the business.

Unfortunately, there are no hard and fast rules to apply here. Each individual case will need to be handled on its own merits and in its own context. I would suggest that if you have the right people in the right positions, there will be fewer times you'll need to be concerned about accommodating special situations. Happy employees tend to stress the system less. I often lean on the Six Human Needs that Tony Robbins promotes, as remembering these emotional connections to life can help a manager provide for employees in a way that keeps them happy, healthy, and a contributing member of the organization.

Tony suggests that every human needs these six things in their life:

- Certainty
- Uncertainty
- Significance
- Connection
- Growth
- Contribution

In the workplace Certainty looks like knowing what to expect every day, and what the paycheck will look like. Uncertainty is that gentle stress that gets us to change. At work, this might be change, improvement, or what the next customer brings in the door.

Significance means we matter, and people appreciate what we do. Your review and recognition program helps support an employee's significance. Connection is the feeling that we are a part of something bigger than ourselves. The inclusivity we spoke of earlier can support this with your employees, as well as things like community involvement, networking events, or having responsibilities assigned that are associated with skill growth or outside interests.

Growth is obvious and often takes the form of training and promotions, but can also be emotional growth, increased responsibilities, or financial growth. Lastly, Contribution might take the form of ideas being implemented, recognition for increasing sales or production, or helping to initiate a major organizational change.

Paying attention to these core needs can help to avoid too many situations where employees are spending less time than they need to at there job. They directly affect your turnover rate and the associated costs.

With that said, there will be times when an employees' life gets in the way of work. Be patient, and recognize that the person needs to come first. Loyalty during difficult times can create an employee that goes above and beyond for you when things calm down in their life.

On the other hand, you will come across those individuals who live in constant drama. These individuals will need more structure, higher levels of accountability, and often take more of your time than they should. Lean on your HR policies for time off, work times, and employee expectations. If you find that the individual is taking advantage of the system, a sit-down meeting to discuss expectations will be required. I suggest a signature on documentation that describes the policy. The next time it becomes an issue, a gentle, verbal reminder of what you'd talked about and they had signed off on. The third time they get written up formally as a warning. If it continues to a fourth or fifth time, termination may need to be considered. This is not personal...it's business.

Pay attention to your staff, accommodate or move staff as needed by their skills and/or weaknesses, ensure set HR policies, grow your coaching skills, and you won't need to fire nearly as many people as you may think. Managing people when you refuse to think of turnover as an option will challenge you—but it will also make you a better manager. Remember, managing requires a different way of thinking.

Chapter 21: Consistency

That brings me to the final attribute I really want you to focus on as you try to become the best manager you can be: Consistency.

A few years back I had spent two full days presenting to the operations staff of a major automotive organization. We had covered topics ranging from creating trust in customers, to service counter operations, to the Customer Buying Process, and selling to the price shopper. At the end of the two days, the head of the organization came to the front of the room to say a few words and unexpectedly asked me to sum up sixteen hours of training in one word. Although I was admittedly caught off guard and hated to choose one word, the most important word from two days of training came immediately to mind: Consistency.

Consistency is everything.

Consistency is everything; consistently good or consistently poor—regardless of whether performance, communication, or any of a million other things—can change an organization irreversibly. So let's be clear: If you want your business to grow sustainably, one of the keys will be your consistency as a manager.

Consistency in everything: Consistency in meetings, in expectations, in accountability, in gratitude (don't forget to praise your team for a job well done), in attitude, in personality.

If you want your business to grow sustainably, one of the keys will be your consistency as a manager.

Seek to be consistent in everything you do. There is little excuse anymore for not holding regular meetings or reviews of everything from facility to expectations. Set a calendar up and create reminders. You will be happy you created such consistency!

When thinking about managing consistently, one of the biggest places managers get themselves in trouble is by playing favorites, whether or not they're even aware they're doing so. After all, we all get along with some people better than we do others—it's only natural. We are human, after all. Being a manager, however, you need to treat everyone equally and put forth that equal treatment in such a way to ensure that nobody can question it.

This, of course, goes back to so many of the things we've talked about in previous chapters, like being objective and not having friends within the organization, developing a clear organizational philosophy and building accountability into everything you do. Policies, processes, and procedures must apply equally to everyone—and you set that tone by being consistent.

Consistency means:

- *You lead by example.*
- *You call others out when they aren't being consistent.*
- *You're accountable to your employees just as they are accountable to you.*
- *You're transparent about why and when you need to do something (such as an expectation of timeliness) differently than your expectation of employees.*

The hard part of being consistent as a shop owner is that this equality thing applies to you as well! If you ask everyone to be ready to work at 8 am but drop the kids off at school around 9 am before coming to work then the optics are not good. The best way to handle this is to be upfront with everyone and let them know that yes, you do come in later, but that part of it is that you trust the organization to get up and running without you every day and that you work later than anyone else in the organization. Being able to drop the kids to school is a benefit of being an owner—but that also means that if you have expectations of your employees to work certain hours, they need to see that you stay late or work other hours. Be transparent so that there is no perception of a double standard, and that should help tremendously.

Don't Wait

Consistency cannot wait; it is essential to setting the tone for your team and ensuring that your management is in-line with the core organizational philosophy. Even if you haven't been consistent with things in the past, start anew today. Set your calendar, set your reminders, and start being consistent. Even picking just one thing to be consistent about will start the habit.

Even if you haven't been consistent with things in the past, start anew today.

Here's the thing: If you can do the same thing for forty days, you can make it a habit. Even if you have to start with one area at a time, you can do it, and you should start today.

A word of caution:

- *When you say you're going to do something, you have to do it.*

- *And you have to keep with it.*
- *This means if you set a policy, procedure, expectation, you have to keep with it.*
- *If you change it in a few weeks, for instance, people will come to realize that you don't mean the changes you've implemented.*
- *If employees develop a "this too shall pass" attitude, you won't get buy-in.*
- *Remember the lessons of previous chapters. Be inclusive as you design policies and processes, and if you do have to make changes, wait until you have appropriate data.*

As mentioned previously, when putting something in place, plan on leaving it there for a while. You want employees to know that you put thought into the new changes and that you mean it when you say something is to be different. Remember the 'J Curve' of change and stick with the ups and downs of the performance metrics. If the plan was good, and you make the modifications necessary to keep things on track, eventually you will see the benefits of the change. Changing your mind and plan too often only teaches employees to ignore you. That's not what you want.

Remember the 'J Curve' of change and stick with the ups and downs of the performance metrics.

So get the buy-in and engagement by making changes right, and then stick to those changes. Be consistent. Be fair. Be good to your employees by being clear, transparent, and just.

Because the flip side is that anything that is consistently bad creates its own set of problems. Things that are consistently bad will ruin your business, even if it does so slowly. And this can be any area where things are consistently bad—any area! Usually, this gets recognized, and in time, fixed, but there are occasions in which a manager's blind spots can get in the way. So again, practice being objective, use data, and practice inclusive decision-making and you'll help avoid those blind spots that can sink a business.

The other thing to watch for? When consistency itself causes problems.

What? I know, I know. I just told you to be consistent in everything. And really, for the most part, you should. You just should also be using data to confirm what you are doing.

See, without regular reviews of your metrics, operations, processes, and observations, you can get what I call consistency drift. You may have a process or procedure that works every time, every day, and has been in place for years. That's the very definition of consistent—but not necessarily in a good way.

The trap comes into play when managers refuse to evaluate whether or not that policy, process, or procedure is still pertinent, can be improved, or should be modified.

Never take anything for granted. Set up times for regular reviews of everything your shop does.

You may need to break this up into sections, and in fact, I would recommend it, so you can really focus on whichever piece you're reviewing. Regardless, put the review sessions on your calendar, set your reminder, and make sure it happens, being sure to include relevant shareholders and department heads as applicable.

Regularly review:

- **People.**
- **Processes.**
- **Marketing activities**.
- **Workflow.**

To review: Consistency within your organization sets a tone for both your employees and your customers. Customers love knowing what to expect when they show up. Employees feel better knowing what to expect throughout the year. Remember the 6 Human Needs according to Tony Robbins. Certainty is the very first one and this translates to consistency.

Consistency within your organization sets a tone for both your employees and your customers.

239

Consistency can be both good and bad, so make sure you know where the consistency is in your organization. Use baby steps, data, inclusive and employee-driven decisions, and consistency to change what needs to be changed in your business.

Conclusion

Hopefully, by now you see the value in not just limiting employee turnover, but also in embracing the attributes and skills of becoming a great manager. If you're at all like me, this isn't what you envisioned when you first became a manager or shop owner— but that doesn't make the skills any less important. Life and business are about growth. Your success in both will be directly attributable to how much effort you put into that growth.

If you not only want to reduce employee turnover but create a truly sustainable organization, you must commit to learning to be a manager. Work on one skill at a time until you feel more comfortable and then move to the next one. Remember, consistently striving to be a good or even great manager means that you will always have to be building, honing, and developing your management skills.

Utilize online training, goal-setting software, instructor-led training, and reading to build your skills. Your organization and employees will benefit greatly from it! If you run into challenges you cannot seem to overcome—ask for help!

The last piece of advice I will offer is that it is better to start something imperfectly than wait for perfect before implementation. Because all things mechanical can be right or wrong, perfect or not, those with a technical background often tend to wait until they have all the bugs worked out of a plan before jumping in and making it happen. This will take more time than you have and will never actually result in perfection as one person can only think of so much!

This is not to say that research, data, and well thought out process are not important, but only that once you've got a plan seventy percent baked, get it out there and let the learning begin. The input you'll gain from users of the new process, procedure, or change will help you to finalize whatever it was you began. Never forget, managing is a journey, and will never be a true destination.

Keep up the great work…and never stop learning!

Addendum 1: Interviewing Skills

Interviewing takes practice. Nobody ever got good at interviewing without doing a lot of it.

The truth is, the more people you interview the better questions you will ask and the better intuition you will have. The more you interview, the more lessons you will learn and the better prepared you will be for future interviews.

Always Be Hiring

Even if you don't need anyone, it's always good to accept applications and be willing to interview promising applicants. For one, it's always far better to know those promising applicants exist and how to contact them, should you need to fill a position on short notice.

This also allows you to get better at interviewing without the pressure of needing to hire. Additionally, you will make better hiring decisions without the pressure, learn who is available in the marketplace, and just generally put a little gentle pressure on your workforce to perform better—as they'll know you're always willing to bring in better talent if you see it.

Interviewing objectives:

- **Assess cultural fit.**
- **Understand how the individual is likely to respond in common organizational scenarios.**
- **Assess skill set and problem-solving ability.**

Know What You Are Looking For

Before you interview any new applicants, have in mind what you are looking for. Have a list of important considerations, and when you look at resumes, be thinking of what follow-up questions you should have at your disposal. Be prepared for each interview.

Know what the important characteristics and skill sets for the job are, and in the interview, be mindful of questions that can help you learn how each interviewee ranks on each skill and characteristic. If part of your managerial responsibilities includes

244

preparing your employees for interviews, train them to interview. Interviewing does not come naturally to everyone, and if someone has never conducted one before, it can be intimidating.

Start each interview on time, and don't rush things. Along those lines, give yourself plenty of time for each interview; even if most interviews only take 15-30 minutes, allowing an hour, for instance, gives you that time for the rare candidates where you might need that extra time.

Principles for a great interview:

- Keep it structured.
- Have specific objectives for each part of the interview.
- Conduct your interviews in more than one place.
- Have interviews conducted by more than one person.

Use the tools at your disposal. That might be personality tests, artificial intelligence assessments, online resources, even video chat (for remote interviewees) and the phone.

Don't just conduct one interview, either, or at the very least, don't just conduct that interview in one place. One of the best ways to get a good sense for who someone truly is and how they might fit in your organizational culture is to see them in different places and different settings.

Similarly, it can be easy for someone to get through one interview. Getting through three of them, though, requires someone really be who they say they are.

Putting people in different physical locations forces them to react to those different environments, such as those environments in which they might work.

Similarly, you can choose environments designed to put them at ease, such as a coffee shop or diner, if you want to make sure they are comfortable and themselves.

A client that I worked with a few years ago (with a very successful shop, I might add...) used this as their interview process:

1. Telephone interview.
2. Off-site interview, usually at a casual dinner.
3. On-site interview, with multiple interviewers.
4. Formal job offer to both the potential employee and their significant other. (Creates more buy-in).

Whatever process you choose, be sure to conduct more than one interview and see the potential candidate in more than one environment.

Picking Questions

If you've had trouble in the past hiring the right people or are not comfortable interviewing, one thing that can help is, well, getting help.

Have others with you to ask questions, write your questions down, read up on interviewing beforehand, and practice on existing personnel.

Similarly, know what you are looking for and design questions based on those attributes, skills, and experience. Past experience will help with this, as will asking current employees what they consider to be the necessary, and important, skills a person should possess. You can even ask what question(s) they would like to see asked in an interview.

Personally, I look for individuals who can demonstrate they are willing to learn, seem as they would be a good fit for the culture of my organization, seem they could help make positive cultural change, and possess the skill set(s) needed by my organization and the position I am trying to fill.

General interviewing questions include:
- Why do you work in this industry?
- Describe a good day for you.
- Describe a really bad day for you.
- What do you do outside of work? Hobbies? Interests? Friends?
- What did you enjoy about your last employer?

These generalized questions—and questions like them—help me get a sense for who people are and how they might fit the culture I want to keep building. When it comes to technicians, I have more specific questions I use, such as:

- What type of work do you most enjoy or are you most passionate about?
- Explain to me your diagnostic process.
- What bothers you most about previous service advisors you've worked with?
- What vehicle do you drive and why?

I also have specific questions I use for service advisors:
- What do you dislike the most about customers?
- What bothers you the most about previous technicians you've worked with?
- If I call your previous employer, what will they tell me about you?

For support personnel, I have a few other questions I always use:
- What makes you think you'd like to work here?
- What did you really like about your last job?
- Tell me about a time when you had to deliver bad news to a customer.

Important No-No Items

There are a few things you cannot ask legally. You cannot ask about race, color, or national origin; you cannot ask about religion; you cannot ask about sex, gender identity, or sexual orientation. You cannot ask about pregnancy status, disability, age, citizenship, marital status (or number of children). There are other questions you probably shouldn't ask, either, such as political beliefs, but the previously mentioned questions are specifically prohibited by law.

Good interviewers:

- *Listen actively.*
- *Take great notes.*
- *Let the interviewee ask questions—and pay attention to those questions.*

Resumes will never tell the whole story of who someone is, which is why good interviewing skills are so important.

Fortunately, interviewing is a skill you can develop.

Preparation is key to a good interview, as is a willingness to hire anytime you see the right candidate. Interview on-site and off, know what you can and should ask just as you know what you cannot and should not ask, and make the best possible use of the time you have. Remember: *Always be hiring!*

Addendum 2: Building Your Onboarding Process

Employee onboarding may sound like a luxury—after all, can't your other employees help new hires get the hang of things?—but the truth is, good onboarding is an essential part of communicating expectations and culture, as well as a necessary part of limiting turnover. There are statistics that suggest employees who participate in an onboarding process remain on the job years longer than those who do not participate in an onboarding process. Want to limit turnover? Have an onboarding process!

Good onboarding is all about setting the right tone for your new hires.

If you can get employees off to the right start, they are far more likely to find job satisfaction and success—and you are far less likely to be disappointed with their work. The "right start" may look different in each organization, and may be somewhat subjective, but have a formal plan will ensure that, whatever a "right start" means in your organization, you'll accomplish it.

The First Thirty Days Are Everything

The first thirty days are everything when it comes to setting the tone and saving yourself later pain, and good hiring makes onboarding easier—yet another reason to always be hiring.

Of course, people with some level of experience in shops like yours can make starting them easier—but you still have to communicate exactly what your expectations are and how accountability in your shop works, and that's where onboarding comes in handy.

Have A Plan, Goals, And Priorities

Before you onboard a new employee, you need a plan for what that onboarding will ideally look like. Not only does a plan help keep you organized when you are onboarding the new hire, but it helps the organization around you know what to expect, too. The more you can codify this, the better; if the new hire also knows what to expect in their onboarding process, all the better.

*Your onboarding plan should have priorities,
goals, and milestones, ideally at
30, 60, and 90 days.*

Not only does setting those priorities and goals ahead of time help hold new employees accountable, but they help hold you and your team accountable, too. If a new hire isn't meeting those milestone goals, everyone involved can examine why not—is it a problem with the new hire's work, or have they simply not been given the skills or tools they need to reach those goals?

Other Considerations

Additionally, it helps to be thorough in your onboarding process. An observational understanding of how every aspect of your business works in concert helps new hires see the larger role their part plays, and it's important you don't rush that, lest you risk not developing that understanding, which is an important part of developing your organizational culture.

*Watching everyone involved—technicians,
receptionists, service, etc—helps new hires gain
a better understanding of how each piece works
in your organizational system, regardless of what
their responsibilities may be.*

Example Plan

Let's look at an example onboarding plan:

Step 1: Before their first day

Even before a new hire's first day, reach out to them and let them know what to expect that first day. Have the service manager or someone else they will be working with closely reach out to say hello. Invite them to a "lunch 'n' learn" before their first day, and use it as an opportunity to simply make introductions so they're familiar with some of the people they'll be working with.

> ***Set up their first day so that new hires are guaranteed success.***

Step 2: Day 1

Ideally, you should set up their first day so that they're guaranteed success. Make it memorable for them, and don't just throw them to the wolves. Regardless of the position they're stepping into, you want to help them get started with easy successes. Keep things simple their first day.

What does that look like? It might mean you simply focus on getting them used to their working environment. Give them a tour of the shop. Schedule a breakfast or lunch for everyone to meet the new employee. Have their email, Slack, voicemail, uniforms, and associated logins ready to go and make sure they're comfortable with each system they'll need to use.

In general, use the first day to focus on observing basic processes.

Focus on ensuring they understand basic processes of the shop. That might be customer intake (forms, greeting, parking), dispatch, where parts come from, and more. This should generally just be observation at this step unless the new hire already has experience with some of these pieces, in which case you can start easing them into the processes. Remember, though, that you want to ensure success as they get started.

One more thing I'd like to point out in this section is that the message you send on that first day becomes important to long-term success. Many organizations will wait to order uniforms, business cards, etc. until the 30, 60, or 90 day mark. This sends a message that "we're not really sure we like you yet." It is far better to set a tone of "we know you'll succeed" and have these things ready to go on the first day.

The message I get when I see an organization hold back uniforms, business cards, etc., is that "we're not sure we know what we're doing when it comes to hiring, so we expect this person to fail." If you focus on your hiring and interviewing process, by the time you are onboarding a new associate, you should have enough confidence to set them up for success. If your process is not such that you can have confidence with your new hire, then going through the entire process again and again is going to cost you much more than uniforms, business cards, and a welcome card!

Step 3: The first week

The first week or two really focus on giving your new hires plenty of structure that they can use as they get comfortable with your processes. The more structure you can provide new hires, the better they will learn your expectations and pick up the skills they need to be successful in your shop.

> **The more structure you can provide new hires, the better they will learn your expectations and pick up the skills they need to be successful in your shop.**

Not only does this structure help keep them from developing bad habits, but it helps them feel more comfortable as they pick up skills and processes. As a result, it can be incredibly helpful to new hires if you assign specific activities at specific times and with specific people who can help mentor them.
Consider this more detailed sample plan below:

Day one
- *7:30 am* Attend breakfast with the owner/manager to discuss the day.

- *8:30 am* Return to the shop for a tour and HR paperwork.
- *10:00 am until 12:00 pm* Shadow Tom at the service counter.

Day two
- *7:30 am* Observe opening procedures.
- *8:00 am* Observe customer greeting and intake.
- *9:00 am* Spend an hour with the owner/manager creating repair orders.
- *10:00 am* Write the next maintenance service repair order at the service counter.

Adapt your plan as necessary.

Checking in regularly is a key to ensuring successful onboarding.

If you aren't communicating regularly with your new hires, you cannot know how they are doing. And if you don't know how they are doing, you can't help troubleshoot any potential problems. As a result, it's essential that you check in with the new hire daily for the first couple of weeks.

I like to keep the following few questions in mind each time I check in, though I vary my questions slightly as needed and as I get to know new hires better.

Consider asking:

- What is working, what is not?
- What needs more practice?
- What questions do you have?

Each new hire will be a bit different, with different experience and skill levels; be adaptable to the needs of each employee. They also may not be fully transparent yet, especially as they are still testing the waters. They will, for instance, feel like there are certain things it's assumed they know, but don't. As they get more comfortable, however, they will ask better questions and be more honest in what is working, and not working for them. Show some patience, and use metrics where you can to evaluate progress or understanding.

Making A Plan

Of course, a big part of making those check-ins effective is tying them to a plan you've built with the new hire. That plan should include goals—SMART goals—and priorities. Set expectations and performance goals for the first 30 days, 60 days, and 90 days. After the first 30 days, you can revise the 60- and 90-day goals, but it's important that you get new hires thinking longer term from the get-go as well.

Want to successfully onboard? Set expectations and performance goals for the first 30, 60, and 90 goals—and revisit and revise as needed at each 30-day point.

Continually review how things are going. After the first 90 days, perhaps you'll move to quarterly reviews—or you may decide that you need to continue reviewing every 30 days. You'll have to make that decision for yourself, based on how the new hire is doing and the needs of your team.

Remember that they probably won't do things just like you—and that that's okay. Good managers hire the best people and get out of their way. When you have new hires, odds are good you hired them because of a skill set or experience; it won't do anyone involved any good if you spend your energy trying to change them.

Onboarding is about working through processes, not about skills, personality, or personal work habits. So focus on process targets.

For instance, these might be service advisor process goals for the first 30 days:

- Understand basic organizational processes
- Answer the phones and take appointments
- Understand the dispatch process
- Be able to estimate and prioritize a basic courtesy inspection

By 60 days, these might be your process goals:

- Be able to estimate and prioritize a basic courtesy inspection
- Be able to write maintenance and basic service repair orders
- Be able to order and receive most parts

And your 90 days process targets might look like this:

- Be able to write all but the most complex of repair orders
- Be able to dispatch work to assigned technicians
- Is now dealing with at least 4 complete repair orders each day (up to 10 maintenance RO's)

You might have other goal targets, too, of course, targets like:

- Number of appointments each day
- Number of RO's written each day
- Hours sold per RO
- Gross profit targets

In order to onboard successfully, keep the following things in mind:

- *Having a plan and structure gets everyone off to a good start.*

- *Setting expectations and goals gives direction and creates habits.*
- *Making onboarding a formal, codified process makes the organization responsible for creating a great employee.*

Index

About The Author

Greg Marchand is an author, industry consultant, and educator. A former shop owner, Toyota business consultant, and college teacher, Greg is passionate about the health and sustainability of the automotive industry. Greg believes that the future of the automotive industry relies on a business's ability to adapt to market demands, deliver quality, learn quickly, and build relationships with all stakeholders.

Greg designs and delivers knowledge rich, engaging automotive service and sales curriculum for instructor led and virtual instructor led training programs delivered throughout the U.S., Canada, and Europe. He also conducts in-shop process consultations worldwide and served as the Special Advisor to the President of Kia Motors Adria Group where he oversaw all aspects of new vehicle distribution, sales, and aftersales support throughout eight Central European countries.

Opportunities to present customer satisfaction and business management programs have allowed Greg to positively influence organizations such as Advance Auto Parts, Midas, Meineke, ASA Colorado, ASA Midwest, IGO North Carolina, Service Maxxx Slovenia, Kia Motors Adria Group, and numerous other automotive service organizations.

His spare time is spent fishing, skiing, and ice climbing.

Markedly Grow Your Gross Profit

Imagine Life, When YOUR Business Has Grown To Where You Want It...

If you are like me and KNOW:
What Got You Here Today,
WILL NOT Get You To
Where You Deserve To Be...

Go To

www.formula4profit.com

And Open The Doors To What Can Be